Renaissance Art
Outside Italy

art horizons

Renaissance Art
Outside Italy

Marilyn Stokstad

Chairman, Department of the History of Art
University of Kansas

WM. C. BROWN COMPANY PUBLISHERS,
Dubuque, Iowa

ART HORIZONS SERIES

Consulting Editor

WILLARD F. WANKELMAN
Bowling Green University

A growing interest in art and art history is evident today in the United States and has created a need for a new approach in the formulation of classroom teaching materials.

The ART HORIZONS SERIES, designed for introductory courses in art appreciation and art history, transmits the excitement of the subject to the student seeking a liberal education. This series offers both the student and teacher flexibility of subject matter as well as authoritative writing in each topic area. Although the individual titles are self-contained, collectively they cover the major subjects usually discussed in an introductory course.

Copyright © 1968 by
Wm. C. Brown Company Publishers

Library of Congress Catalog Card Number: 68–14577

Printed in U. S. A.

preface

During the fifteenth and sixteenth centuries throughout Europe, artists and philosophers were rediscovering man and the world around him; however, whereas the Italian artist saw man as a complete and self-sufficient individual, the northern artist saw him, in spite of his earthly pride and splendor, as a creature of God and only a speck in the universe. Medieval intellectualism and emotionalism continued in the fifteenth century in the artist's intense observation of nature and in his determination to express spiritual values through physical objects. Christian concepts were represented in tangible, realistic terms, nonetheless potent because of their disguised nature. With eye and hand trained to the exacting work of manuscript illumination, the fifteenth-century northern artist recorded the world with a wealth of realistic detail. Light, indicating the presence of the Creator of the universe, was the artist's concern, and he recorded its minutest gradations and fluctuations. Thus, the northerner soon mastered the art of landscape painting and the representation of the surfaces of material objects. In contrast, the Italian artist, who was more concerned with art theory, concentrated on the mathematical rather than the visual representation of space. The northern artist, in spite of his skill in the representation of the physical world and its occupants, still saw every detail as symbolic of the Christian religious and philosophical system. He remained as concerned with making the invisible visible as the Medieval artist had been.

Renaissance Art Outside Italy has been chosen as the title of this book in preference to the usual designation "The Northern Renaissance" in order to justify the inclusion of Spain and France as well as the Low Countries, Germany, and England. The Flemish School is discussed in greater detail than the other schools; however, this seemed appropriate considering the dominant influence of the art of the Low Countries on the rest of Europe during the fifteenth century. The present book is unusual both in the breadth of geographical coverage and in the inclusion of sculpture and architecture as well as painting.

Renaissance Art Outside Italy was written for the person who wants more information than can be included in a world history of art but does not have ready access to a number of monographs on individual artists. The present book should be considered a summary outline and a guide for further study. As an aid to student travellers, the city in which a work of art is now located is indicated in parentheses after the first appearance of the name in the text. If the date of the work is not mentioned elsewhere in the text, it is included in these parentheses.

The author wishes to thank Sally Shultz, Robert Mowry, and Robert Leider for their invaluable assistance in the preparation of this manuscript.

contents

1

The International Style

Art in western Europe at the end of the fourteenth century was created for aristocratic patrons and reflected the international character of the society. A painting from Bohemia or France had the same decorative, linear quality and meticulous rendering of detail as one produced in Spain or England. Artists and patrons looked back to the rapidly disappearing world of the Gothic cathedral, of chivalry, of the courtly romance, and their paintings, tapestries, and books showed no signs of the social and political unrest sweeping Europe. The collapse of the feudal system, the rise of the middle class, the death and destruction caused by the Hundred Years War, and the succession of plagues which swept Europe were not reflected in the art of the fourteenth century. The religious crises culminating in the split of the papacy and the establishment of the papal court at Avignon (1309–1377, 1378–1418), however, did play an important role in the development of the fourteenth-century style. In the new palace at Avignon, Italian and French artists worked together on the decorations. The French love of elegant, linear abstractions and concern with the details of nature were reinforced by the Sienese tendency toward grace and decorative qualities in painting. The resulting synthesis is called the International Style.

The International Style was a precious, courtly art in which realism was combined with decorative effects. This decorative quality was emphasized by bright colors, the rhythmic play of lines, richness of surface effects, and an unerring feeling for abstract designs in the rendering of details and in the organization of the total picture plane. At the same time, the artists were beginning to observe the world with great care and to record appearances of objects and beings with a new accuracy. This realism was limited to the details of nature; however, a sense of space was achieved in the architectural settings and, occasionally, in the representations of crowds. Landscapes tended to remain

1

tapestry-like collections of plants and fantastic rocks. The fourteenth-century artist seemed intuitively aware that there was a system of space and light in nature but he failed to develop any logical artistic representation. Light was used to accentuate forms, but no single light source was used. A coherent representation of light and space was to be the great achievement of the fifteenth century.

Radical tendencies in the International Style were first seen in manuscript illumination, especially in the manuscripts produced for John, Duke of Berry, who was one of the greatest art patrons of all time. The artists working for him studied light, space, atmosphere, the visual appearance of all the details of nature. They paved the way for the Flemish masters of the fifteenth century. The most famous artists working in the court of Berry were the Limbourg brothers. They were not unique, however. Their two greatest predecessors were Andre Beauneveu (*ca.* 1316–*ca.* 1402) and Jacquemart de Hesdin (died 1409).

In the twenty-four full-page illustrations of prophets and apostles which he painted for the *Psalter of the Duke of Berry* (Paris), Beauneveu for the first time created three-dimensional rather than linear forms. He realized that light fell from a single source, and in his representation of draperies and faces, his study of shadows approaches true chiaroscuro modelling. He continued his study of space with accurate linear perspective in the thrones of the prophets, but he returned to Medieval tradition in his use of diapered blue backgrounds for the figures and decorative floral borders for the illuminations. Jacquemart de Hesdin, a Fleming, continued Beauneveu's study of space and light. In his finest books of hours, such as the *Brussels Hours* (Brussels, 1402), the realistic portraits of the Duke and members of the court, the depiction of the elegant costume of the time, and the realistic portrayal of the castles, cities, and the landscape of France are especially remarkable.

The culmination of the International Style in book illustration was a book of hours known as the *Très Riches Heures* (Chantilly) by the Limbourg brothers, Jean, Pol, and Herman (active 1390–1416). The Limbourgs appeared first about 1390 in Paris as goldsmiths, but in 1401 or 1402, Pol was in Burgundy and, by 1413, all three were working in Berry, where they succeeded Jacquemart de Hesdin as court painters. The *Très Riches Heures* contained a calendar of the months and the prayers for the canonical hours. The hours were done between 1402 and 1410; the calendar was a little later, 1411–1416. One of the most interesting aspects of the manuscript is the detailed study by the artists of the French countryside. In the calendar, the labors of the months were represented as scenes of daily life in carefully observed landscape settings. Thus, the paintings in the *Très Riches Heures* are an important source for the study of life in the fifteenth century. *February* is a genre scene of peasants warming themselves in front of a fire (Fig. 1). The gray skies and barren landscape, the snow on buildings and trees, the feeling of bitter cold are all recorded. The landscape was represented by overlapping planes, as in the Medieval tradition, and yet the figures were organized in a three-dimensional space. Buildings, such as Notre Dame, Paris, and even whole cities were included. Light was studied not only in full sunshine but at twilight. In the representation of interiors, a feeling of space was achieved through the placement of furniture; however, the perspective space-box seen in Italian art was not yet used. The artists dwelt on genre aspects, picturesque figures with tattered clothes, as well as the luxury of kings and nobles. The paintings remain appropriate manuscript illuminations; that is, they are essentially surface designs. Even when they open into space, a decorative frame was used to bring the eye back to the surface of the page. The success of a manuscript illumination depends on its two-dimensional quality, and when the representation of three-dimensional space reached the stage used by the Limbourg brothers, the artist and his patrons were ready to turn to panel painting.

Figure 1. The Limbourg Brothers, *February* from *Les Très Riches Heures du Duc de Berry* (1411–1416), Musée Condé, Chantilly, France. Photo: Giraudon.

The leading panel painter at the turn of the century was Melchior Broederlam (active *ca.* 1380–1409). He was court painter to a brother of John of Berry, Philip the Bold, Duke of Burgundy. About 1394, Broederlam painted his masterpiece, the wings for an altarpiece carved by Jacques de Barye. The paintings of the Dijon Altarpiece (Fig. 2) had as their subjects the Annunciation, Visitation, Presentation, and Flight into Egypt; however, the meaning of the paintings went beyond the simple stories which first meet the eye. Broederlam developed a hidden symbolism in which complex ideas were disguised as everyday events and objects. For example, the temple behind Mary in the Annunciation was meant to signify by its contrast between Romanesque and Gothic architecture the contrast of old and new and, by extension, the theme of Judaism versus Christianity. The Romanesque style was considered "old fashioned," foreign, Oriental, or Jewish, and thus was equated with the Old Law. The Gothic or modern style referred to the New Law and Christianity. The three windows, the three gables, and the three lamps in the building symbolized the Trinity; Mary both sat in and was the new church or the temple of the Trinity.

Figure 2. Melchior Broederlam, Dijon Altarpiece, *Annunciation* and *Visitation* (1394–1399), 64 × 51″, Museum of Dijon, France. Photo: Studio R. Remy.

The Dijon Altarpiece is the work of an artist whose sense of realism was strong, yet who was bound by conventions. The compositions were adapted to the irregular, Medieval form of the altar, and yet the paintings themselves were three-dimensional and almost atmospheric. Interior and exterior settings were combined by the removal of the walls of the buildings and, in both architecture and landscape, a recession into space was implied by an axial perspective in which lines converged on a central axis rather than at a single point. The figures were bulky volumes in space, even casting shadows at last. Their movements were quite natural, yet their drapery was represented as linear and mannered, and they remain definitely in the foreground plane. A new warmth appeared in the colors, especially in the earth colors of the landscape, and a unified sense of light added to the atmospheric effects created by the artist. In spite of the realism, the feeling for convergence of lines, the observation of natural detail, and the convincing figures, Medieval devices such as stylized rock forms for mountains and a gold background were retained. The conflict in Broederlam's style is epitomized by his depiction of a realistic hawk flying in a sky of gold.

The growing interest in realism and the rise of popularity of painting on panels led to the development of the portrait as an independent subject. The first surviving portrait on panel is that of *John the Good* (Paris) by an anonymous artist about 1370. The painting is hardly a masterpiece from the aesthetic standpoint, but it is an important historical document, recording accurately the appearance of the King of France. The King's head and shoulders were represented in profile against a neutral background. The profile view was preferred by Gothic artists for a variety of reasons. The profile had distinct decorative possibilities in the curl of hair and outline of features. It depended more on silhouette or the linear pattern of the face than on modelling and, thus, was congenial to an essentially two-dimensional art of surface patterns. Finally, the turning of the face, and especially eyes, away from the spectator set up a psychological distance desired by a society which still saw man as a symbol rather than as an individual.

The International Style was not confined to painting but was also found in the tapestries, metalwork, ivory carving, and other arts of the fourteenth and early fifteenth century. Tapestries, for example, were much more plentiful than paintings. Charles V of France had in his inventory 200 tapestries in contrast to about twenty pictures. In spite of the requirements of weaving, which demand a simple design and angular contours, the craftsmen were able to create varying effects of light, color, and surface realism while preserving the overall decorative pattern and abstract two-dimensional design appropriate to a wall hanging.

Metal and enamel work, exquisite examples of the jeweler's art, illustrate the refinement and richness of the luxury arts at the beginning of the Renaissance. Yet it is painting, and especially panel painting, that must occupy our attention, for it is in this medium that the greatest artists of the century created a new vision of man and his world.

2

The Founders
of the Flemish School of Painting

THE FLEMISH STYLE AND TECHNIQUE OF PAINTING

The great school of Flemish painting in the fifteenth century had its origins in the work of four men—Hubert and Jan van Eyck, Robert Campin, and Roger van der Weyden. During the first half of the century, they created a style which combined the intricate Late Gothic subject matter, emphasizing the symbolic meaning of natural objects or everyday activities, with the new Renaissance interest in representing the physical appearance of the world. The northern artists' paintings still reflected the deep piety of the Middle Ages. The painters did not, at once, begin to study the structure as well as the surfaces of objects, nor did they attempt at first to relate these tangible objects to each other in a unified space. Only gradually did a concern with visual problems, the representation of space, and the appearance of nature become as important as the symbolic meanings of the subject to the artist outside Italy.

Flemish artists of this period were technical innovators, and in the development of oil painting, they made one of the great contributions to the history of art. Jan van Eyck has been called the inventor of oil painting, but this is not strictly true. Painting with an oil medium had been used before the fifteenth century where greater durability was required or when the painting might be exposed to inclement weather. The Flemish artists recognized the great possibilities for richness of color and subtlety of shading inherent in oil as a medium for their pigments and developed the technique for panel painting. The panel was carefully prepared with a gesso ground much as had been done for tempera painting. Then the pigments were mixed with oil rather than egg as a medium. The slower drying oil could be blended, allowing colors to flow into one another, thus permitting a realistic modelling of forms through subtle variation in tone. The colors were built up in a series of semitransparent glazes that permitted a greater intensity and luminosity. The painters welcomed the greater flexibility and freedom as well as the brilliant color effects which were now possible in oil painting, and the new medium was adopted rapidly.

THE SCHOOL OF BRUGES AND GHENT: HUBERT AND JAN VAN EYCK

Acknowledged leader of the Flemish School was Jan van Eyck (*ca.* 1390–1441). Nothing is known of his early life, although he was probably trained in the manuscript workshops of Flanders. His career as an artist and courtier is recorded in scattered references in contemporary documents. From 1422 to 1424, he worked for John of Bavaria in the Hague, and on May 19, 1425, he went to Lille as painter and *valet de chambre* of Philip the Good, Duke of Burgundy. Throughout his life, he was Philip's confidante and ambassador; for example, in 1427 and 1428, he travelled to Spain and Portugal, and he made other "secret" voyages. Thus, Jan van Eyck was not just a painter but a man of affairs, a skilled diplomat and courtier, a man of considerable importance and prestige. Of his personal life, we know only that about 1430 he settled in Bruges, married a girl named Margaret, and subsequently had ten children. His motto was "As I can." He died on July 9, 1441.

The altarpiece of the *Adoration of the Holy Lamb* (Figs. 3 and 4), painted for the Church of San Bavon in Ghent, provides a logical starting place for the study of the art of the Van Eycks. Hubert van Eyck (died 1426) remains a shadowy figure, in spite of his younger brother's admiration for him. In the inscription on the frame of the Ghent Altarpiece (Ghent, 1425–1432), Jan credited Hubert with being the greatest artist of the time,

The painter, Hubert van Eyck, to whom none is deemed superior, began this work, and Jan, who is second to him in art, finished it. Jodocus Vyt paid for it. He invites you by this verse to come and contemplate the great work on the 6th day of May, 1432.

The altarpiece was commissioned by the mayor of Ghent, Jodocus Vyt, from Hubert van Eyck in 1425. Jan assembled it after Hubert's death and completed it by 1432. The theme of the original commission was that of all the saints adoring the Mystic Lamb, a popular late Medieval subject taken from *Revelations* and also based on the visions of St. Hildegard, a twelfth-century German mystic. The sacrificial Lamb of God stands on an altar from which spring the Four Rivers of Paradise. Apostles and Martyrs stand at the right, Patriarchs and Prophets, at the

Figure 3. Hubert and Jan van Eyck, The Ghent Altarpiece, Interior (completed 1432), 11'3" × 14'5", St. Bavon, Ghent, Belgium. Photo: Copyright A.C.L., Brussels.

left; Holy Virgins fill the landscape on the upper right, and Confessors, the upper left. In the altarpiece as it now appears, God is attended by the Madonna and St. John the Baptist and adored by a choir of angels; Adam and Eve frame the composition. On the exterior wings the Annunciation, the donors, and the two St. Johns are represented. The unrelated sizes and shapes of the panels suggest that Hubert had three commissions—an All Saints painting with wings, a retable honoring St. John the Baptist, and a pair of organ shutters with musical angels. Jan could have reworked Hubert's paintings after his death and assembled them into one altarpiece, adding Adam and Eve. Jan very likely painted the entire exterior of the altarpiece.

The central panel, or *Adoration of the Holy Lamb*, reflects the International Style in its rising foreground plane and detailed representation of plants, clothing, and jewelry. An abrupt change takes place, however, in the representation of space in the upper part of the painting where a distant landscape is shown in accurate aerial perspective and the processions of saints are integrated into the setting. Jan van Eyck must have painted this background and probably reworked the lower area to give continuity to the painting. In the lower panels, the scenes of pilgrims and warrior saints led by St. Christopher reflect Hubert's work in their two-dimensional quality; however, Jan has repainted the faces and added a rocky background, palms, and orange trees.

In the upper section of the altarpiece, the impressive triad of God, the Madonna, and St. John the Baptist must have been painted by Hubert as a single unit. To a background which remains spaceless in spite of the rich sculptural modelling, Jan added a sophisticated surface finish. The microscopic realism of the detail is almost incredible. The surrounding musical angels approach genre studies of a choir. While the paintings were evidently conceived as two-dimensional compositions, the lower areas have been reworked in perspective. The full three-dimensional modelling of individual figures is in the style of Jan van Eyck. Finally, Adam and Eve must have been painted entirely by him, since the artist shows a complete control of perspective and chiaroscuro modelling in their representation not found elsewhere on the interior panels. Adam and Eve stand in niches, seen from below. Adam is not idealized but obviously studied from the nude. The artist has given careful attention to details such as the slight change of color in hands and face and the texture of skin and hair. On the other hand, Eve represents the ideal female form in the fifteenth century with her slouching, Late Gothic pose and pear-like form.

The exterior of the altarpiece is devoted to the Annunciation, the two St. Johns, and the donors (Fig. 4). The Annunciation takes place entirely in an interior setting; the room is represented in perspective and a back window opens on a vista of a city. The Madonna is an ordinary girl whose state of beatitude is indicated by a streaming light. The volumes of her body are both enhanced and obscured by the rhythmic, angular drapery forms characteristic of Jan's work. Below the Annunciation are intense, fascinating portraits of the donors, whose solidly painted forms are defined by a single light source. The portrait as an independent type did not exist in the Middle Ages, and the first portraits were donor portraits. Jan van Eyck established a new method of representing his subject, the three-quarter view. By turning the sitter toward the spectator, a psychological contact is established, in contrast to the more decorative and abstract profile portrait in use earlier. The remarkable figures of St. John the Baptist and St. John the Evangelist are portrayed as unpainted sculpture in niches. Such a representation, while consistent with modern taste, was a striking innovation in the fifteenth century.

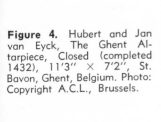

Figure 4. Hubert and Jan van Eyck, The Ghent Altarpiece, Closed (completed 1432), 11'3" × 7'2", St. Bavon, Ghent, Belgium. Photo: Copyright A.C.L., Brussels.

The Ghent Altarpiece, then, seems to be the creation of two different artists representing two different styles. Hubert van Eyck was an exponent of the International Style; Jan van Eyck was a prophet of the achievements to come in the fifteenth century. Hubert van Eyck was a conservative artist working in the Gothic idiom, creating spaceless paintings where elegant weightless figures dressed in costumes of incredible richness float in a landscape made up of decorative foliage patterns. On the other hand, Jan van Eyck was one of the great innovators in the history of art. His paintings dominate the imagination of artists for the rest of the century. Jan van Eyck is one of the few artists to achieve a harmonious balance between the representation of specific details and the synthesis of these details into a coherent pictorial whole. He observed the world with the detachment of a scientist, and in his paintings, he deliberately suppressed both emotion and physical movement. His paintings are cold, analytical, and descriptive, yet under this surface realism are represented not only individuals but physical and psychological types. The objective recording of the visual world was made to serve the most complex religious symbolism. It is Jan van Eyck who carried to the extreme the northern mystical attitude, the northern desire for elaborate, intricate, disguised symbolism, and the northern pantheistic interest in natural details.

The *Annunciation* (Washington, D. C., Fig. 5) is probably an early work. The event takes place in a church whose Romanesque and Gothic architecture indicates the contrast between Old and New Testaments; even the stained glass window and the tiles in the floor foretell the coming of Christ. The Madonna is completely out of scale with the architecture behind her and, thus, symbolically identified with the Church; that is, she *is* The Church, as Bride of Christ, Queen of Heaven, and the means by which God became flesh. The subtlety of this disguised symbolism, an amazing visual record of an unseen happening, is characteristic of Jan van Eyck. Characteristic, too, is the monumental quality even in a tiny painting, the suppression of physical action or emotion, and the complete artistic control of detail, space, and light.

The *Madonna of Chancellor Rolin* (Paris, Fig. 6) is a mature work dated about 1433–1434. The prime minister of Burgundy and the Queen of Heaven are juxtaposed—secular and mundane on the one side, religious and ideal on the other. The artist's contrast of real and

ideal is enhanced by his use of two light sources, the one a natural light from the horizon, the second an otherworldly light illuminating the confronted figures. In this light, the face of Rolin is so detailed that it almost lacks substance. The portrait of the Chancellor is done with careful attention to physical appearance, and yet there is no psychological contact established with him as a man. The faces of the Madonna and Child are so idealized that they become simple, ovoid forms. In this mature, monumental style, the figures are almost overly static. The Madonna is a monumental, throne-like figure, although her drapery falls about her in decorative, linear, angular folds. The richness of detail and warm glowing colors are truly amazing, and yet every detail is unified in terms of the

Figure 5. Jan van Eyck, *The Annunciation* (ca. 1430), 36½ × 14⅜", National Gallery of Art, Washington, D.C., Andrew Mellon Collection.

realistic overall modelling light. The architecture forms a frame for the figures rather than remaining an independent background. The vista dividing the two sides of the room is a masterpiece of landscape painting. Hills, the river, buildings, the crowd, boats, and horsemen are all included and seen through a triple window, the symbol of the

Figure 6. Jan van Eyck, *Madonna of Chancellor Rolin* (1433–1434), 26 × 24½″, The Louvre, Paris, France. Photo: Giraudon.

Trinity. The city below may be the heavenly Jerusalem, and the river, the River of Living Waters. The Garden of Paradise, enclosed by a parapet, is filled with such symbols of the Virgin as the gladiola and the peacock. Thus, this painting is more than the traditional donor portrait. In it the secular and religious, the real and ideal worlds are contrasted.

A similar mood and style can be seen in the famous *The Marriage of Giovanni Arnolfini and Giovanna Cenami* (London, Fig. 7), painted in the same year, 1434. The bride and groom join hands, the groom raises his free hand in the classic gesture of oath taking. This painting is their marriage certificate, and the artist has used a typical bourgoise interior, with figures modelled by a realistic light to disguise the true ·meaning of the painting. A curiously concentrated effect is achieved by focusing Arnolfini's glance on the spectator. In the mirror, surrounded by ten scenes of the Passion of Christ, Van Eyck painted himself with another witness in the doorway, and then signed on the wall behind the couple, "Jan van Eyck was here." The chandelier holding the wedding candle is the eye of God; the dog symbolizes marital fidelity. Van Eyck again used his favorite composition: the symmetrical placement of two major figures with a space opening up between them filled with intricate, realistically represented objects or landscape. His earlier paintings are related to the International Style in their complexity, delicacy, linear quality, and surface elaboration. His mature works became more severe, more sculptural, and spatial relations are completely studied. In this wedding portrait, he is conscientiously monumental and achieves a clarity of space and volume far beyond any of his contemporaries.

THE SCHOOL OF TOURNAI: ROBERT CAMPIN AND ROGER VAN DER WEYDEN

The paintings of Robert Campin and Roger van der Weyden stand in marked contrast with those of Jan van Eyck. These artists were the leaders of the School of Tournai and produced the most popular art of the fifteenth century. The distinctive character of the School of Tournai may be accounted for by the social and religious environment. Whereas Jan van Eyck had aristocratic patrons, Robert Campin and Roger van der Weyden worked for the middle classes. Their commissions came from cities and guilds. Their art is more emotional, their symbolism is relatively easy to understand, and they created a broad style aimed at popular appeal.

Robert Campin (*ca.* 1380–1444), also known as the Master of Flémalle, is a key figure in the break from the International Style in the fifteenth century. His origins are obscure, as are the Van Eycks', and his relationship to them is unknown. Robert was a master painter in Tournai in 1406. He became a citizen of Tournai in 1410; he was a member of the town council, and he led a popular uprising. In 1423, he was dean of the painters' guild, but later he was banished. After a pilgrimage to St. Gilles, he returned to Tournai where he remained until his death.

Figure 7. Jan van Eyck, *The Marriage of Giovanni Arnolfini and Giovanna Cenami* (1434), 33 × 22½". Reproduced by courtesy of The Trustees, The National Gallery, London, England.

Campin's masterpiece is the Merode Altarpiece (New York, Fig. 8). The theme is the Annunciation which takes place in a domestic setting with the donors, the Englebrecht family, kneeling in the garden at the left, and St. Joseph working in his carpenter shop at the right. The three panels are united by the architectural setting, a new achievement in the representation of interior and exterior space. Jan van Eyck may have seen the Merode Altarpiece when he visited Tournai in 1427 and may have been influenced by the painting in his composition for the exterior of the Ghent Altarpiece.

Robert Campin's direct, naive symbolism has great charm, and his painting has a robust quality that belies the mystical subject matter; for example, St. Joseph is building mousetraps to catch the devil, a reference to a popular Medieval tale. Mary sits on the floor, emphasizing her humility, in front of a carved bench whose lion armrests refer to the throne of Solomon. The painting is filled with symbols of the Virgin—lilies, towels, vase, basin, candle, and candlestick. The Incarnation is represented literally, through a round window rays of light support an embryonic Christ carrying the Cross.

Robert Campin's portraits, for example the Englebrechts, were not penetrating psychological studies as were those of Jan van Eyck. Unlike Van Eyck and Van der Weyden, who turned their sitters to the light, Campin often left the features in shadow and had the light fall on the side of the face. This pose increased the sense of solidity of form but reduced the psychological contact with the spectator. When he painted independent portraits, Campin used the three-quarter view, placing the head rather high and adding hands in the corner. This form of bust portrait became the usual type in the fifteenth century.

Robert Campin was fascinated by the play of light over objects. He learned to give forms the appearance of greater solidity than had hitherto been achieved by Flemish artists. The sculptural quality of his painting is such that one assumes he must have known Claus Sluter's work (see Chapter 5). Campin's handling of drapery and emphasis on the faces is similar to Sluter's technique. In spite of his excellent representation of individual forms, Campin had difficulties in organizing his picture as a whole. His compositions are cluttered and often two-dimensional, for he did not master foreshortening or linear perspective and, thus, he seldom succeeded in creating an impression of deep space. In spite of this deficiency, Robert Campin had a greater influence on European painting than did Jan van Eyck. His paintings were easier to understand, and his style was much easier to master.

Fourth of the founders of the Flemish School was Roger van der Weyden (ca. 1400–1464). The first document concerning him may have

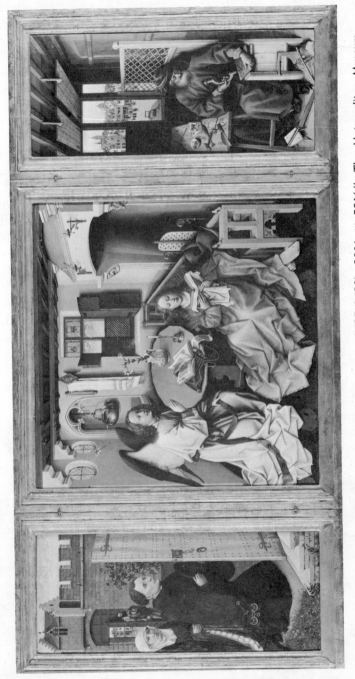

Figure 8. Robert Campin, The Merode Altarpiece (ca. 1425–1428), 29⅜ × 58½″, The Metropolitan Museum of Art, The Cloisters Collection, Purchase, New York.

been the registration of a man named Roger as an apprentice to Robert Campin in 1427. Roger van der Weyden became a master of the painters' guild in 1432 and, in 1436, became official painter of the city of Brussels. He may have made a pilgrimage to Italy in 1450. Roger van der Weyden was the ideal gentleman painter—gracious, poised, with a quality of nobility in his work. He was more copied than any other Flemish master and even influenced Dürer in Germany. His paintings are not signed or dated, thus, the reconstruction of his career is hypothetical.

Van der Weyden's early paintings seem to refer back to Gothic sculpture in their abstraction, their rhythmic organization, and in their use of a shallow, stage-like space. The figures are emphasized and carry the full expressive and intellectual significance of the painting with settings, whether architectural or landscape, subservient to them. Both interior and exterior space is clearly defined in a series of distinct horizontal planes, an opening up of the Gothic stage space into a Renaissance progression of parallel planes in depth. Figures and settings, two- and three-dimensional compositions are united by the linear movements of forms. The compositions are essentially two-dimensional and

Figure 9. Roger van der Weyden, *Descent from the Cross* (before 1434), 7'-2⅝" × 8'7⅛", The Prado, Madrid, Spain.

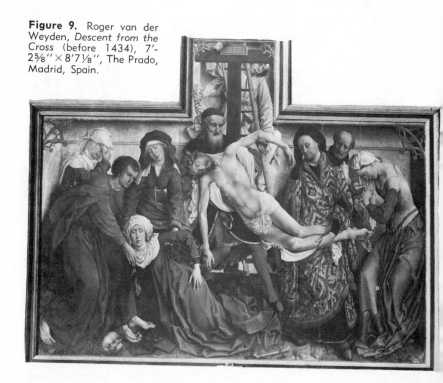

dominated by the surface patterns. The finest example of this style is the *Descent from the Cross* (Madrid, Fig. 9), commissioned in Louvain before 1436 by the archers' guild. Van der Weyden imitated a retable with wooden background and painted frame within which the figures are placed. The color is subtle and controlled, essentially neutral in tone, with blue, white, greenish lavenders, gold brocade, and a dry red in varying shades predominating. The colors are used more for their emotional than for their decorative effects. Van der Weyden's real genius lay in his skill as a designer, and while many of his effects are self-conscious, one can but admire the way in which every form and line is interrelated. Figures are often off-balance, in poses impossible to hold, but perfect from the point of view of abstract design. The arbitrary, flat design is contrasted with the realistic detail of garments, hands, and faces. The power of Van der Weyden's paintings comes in these faces, each of which expresses an intense individual emotion.

Gradually, Van der Weyden's style became more monumental and severe. At the same time, he invented many new motifs which spread throughout Europe, for example, a single landscape which ran through all three wings of a triptych and included the donors as actors in the drama. The swooning Virgin was another of Van der Weyden's innovations. His elegant angels with decorative fluttering garments silhouetted in the sky seem a self-conscious return to the International Style, but when they are used in scenes such as the Crucifixion, they heighten the emotional intensity through their contrast with stark tragedy.

The masterpiece of his middle period is the *Last Judgment* Altarpiece (Beaune, Fig. 10), painted for the hospital founded in Beaune

Figure 10. Roger van der Weyden, The Last Judgment Altarpiece (dedicated 1451), approximately 18 feet wide, Hospital, Beaune, France. Photo: Giraudon.

by Chancellor Rolin in 1443. The chapel with the altarpiece was dedicated in 1451. The triptych, eighteen feet across, is the largest panel painting in northern Europe in the fifteenth century. On the exterior are the
Annunciation, Saints Sebastian and Anthony, and the donors; all nine
panels of the interior are filled with the Last Judgment. God is seated
on a rainbow above St. Michael weighing the souls. The Resurrection
is not represented as an anonymous mass of figures, but as a series of
individuals. No devils are represented; men fall from the weight of
their own sins. The intercessors, Mary and St. John, are far from Christ
and play a small role. Van der Weyden implies that the fate of man
is a result of his own actions. The altarpiece was evidently executed
with the help of assistants, for, although the conception is grand, the
quality of individual details varies considerably.

After 1450, when he may have gone to Rome for the Jubilee, Van
der Weyden's work mellowed. His style had greater breadth, his paintings greater intimacy, richness of color, and softer lights. The Columba
Altarpiece (Munich, Fig. 11) is such a painting. Many art historians
consider this work to be Van der Weyden's masterpiece and the sum-
mation of all his interests. The painting is a triptych with the Adoration,
Annunciation, and Presentation. In the center panel, the Adoration of
the Magi, Van der Weyden painted Charles the Bold of Burgundy as
the youthful Magus; thus, living figures are fully integrated into a
religious painting. The melancholy and pensive mood, a foreboding of
the Crucifixion, is unusual in an Epiphany. On the central pier, over
the Madonna and Child, is placed a crucifix.

Figure 11. Roger van der Weyden, The Columba Altarpiece (1465),
54 × 115″, Bavarian State Painting Collection, Munich, Germany.

The composition shows all of Van der Weyden's skill in producing a highly geometric design, a pattern of verticals and parallel planes with symmetrically placed figures and buildings in a stratified landscape. Van der Weyden enlivens the regularity of the pattern with many slight variations. The Virgin, for example, is slightly off-center. One senses the elegant linear arabesque of a two-dimensional composition lying over a grid of verticals and horizontals all against and in a firmly stratified space. The Annunciation follows the composition established in his earlier paintings but is corrected and improved in every detail. Every object is in perfect accord; the figures are balanced against each other and against the setting. The Presentation is linked to the center panel both by repetition of the interior of the building at the right and by the unifying surface pattern. The Columba Altarpiece was a source of motifs for artists throughout the century.

Roger van der Weyden originated a new form of portrait, the diptych composed of a donor with the Madonna and Child. The Madonna is the type seen in his major paintings—idealized, sweet, simple beauty. The donor portrait is enigmatic and withdrawn, looking into the light against a plain and dark background, with only the eyes and hands emphasized. Sitters are not painted as individuals, but as aristocratic, refined, haughty types. Hundreds of these diptychs were produced by Van der Weyden's shop and by his followers. They served to establish this artist's idealized style throughout northern Europe.

3

Flemish Painting in the Second Half of the Fifteenth Century

THE SECOND GENERATION OF FLEMISH PAINTERS

By the middle of the fifteenth century, young artists adopted the style and technique of the Van Eycks, Robert Campin, and Roger van der Weyden in such numbers that a school of Flemish painting may be said to have been established. The younger painters tended to limit their studies, concentrating on the representation of light or space or the physical appearance of man and nature.

Painters of Flanders in the second half of the fifteenth century may be divided into two schools—the followers of Jan van Eyck and the followers of Roger van der Weyden. The painters of the Eyckian school, such as Petrus Christus and Dirk Bouts, were concerned with problems of representing space, especially solid objects in space. They combined this interest in space with the realistic detail of van Eyck and the expressive qualities, simplifications, and iconography of Van der Weyden. The latter group continued to paint in a popular, somewhat sentimental, vein which led to the quiet beauty of the *détente* style at the turn of the century.

Petrus Christus (*ca.* 1415–1472) has been called a student of Jan van Eyck; however, he did not arrive in Bruges until two years after Van Eyck's death and at first was equally influenced by Roger van der Weyden. In his early work, landscapes were borrowed from Van Eyck and themes and figures from Van der Weyden; however, compositions were simplified and the figures were isolated in space. The principal interest of the artist seems to have been the study of perspective and the integration of the object or figure into its environment.

Petrus Christus came to depend more and more on the paintings of Jan van Eyck, and, after the middle of the fifteenth century, his

tyle became totally Eyckian. The masterpiece of his mature period is
he Legend of Sts. Eligius and Godeberta (New York, Fig. 12). This
ainting of their patron saint was commissioned by the Antwerp gold-
miths' guild. In it, Petrus Christus represented a couple ordering a
vedding ring from St. Eligius. This obvious symbolism only suggests
he intricate iconography worked out by Jan van Eyck and Robert
Campin. Evidently, Petrus Christus' real enthusiasm was for the painting
f still life details such as the crowded shelves and counter which are
lmost incredibly tangible. This love of still life painting led to his
nost original contribution—the portrait in which the sitter was placed
n a definite environment, usually the corner of a carefully depicted
paneled room. Although his style of portrait painting was generally
lerived from Jan van Eyck, Christus painted with a new sense of
olidity. His forms are so simplified that even faces are turned into
:ubist-like ovoids. The portrait in a precise interior is an important
nnovation by Petrus Christus, but his simplification of the features and
iis lack of interest in psychology indicate that he was a lesser artist
han Jan van Eyck.

    Another artist of the second half of the century influenced by both
[an van Eyck and Roger van der Weyden was Dirk Bouts (*ca.* 1415–
1475). The first known works by Bouts date from 1442. By 1445, he
was in Brussels working for Van der Weyden, and he settled in Louvain

Figure 12. Petrus Christus,
*The Legend of Sts. Eligius
and Godeberta* (1449), The
Lehman Collection, New York.

by 1457. Bouts concentrated on achieving a systematic one-point perspective in his painting. While both Jan van Eyck and the Master of Flémalle contrasted an interior box of space with a distant landscape, Dirk Bouts attempted to create a continuous recession into space. Bouts had a deep feeling for nature. Unfortunately, he worked in a period before landscape alone was an appropriate subject for the artist. In his paintings, he established a stage space with a road leading through a deep space defined by various promontories and finally ending in a bluish haze on the horizon. He was not interested in man, and his figures are stiff and awkward and stocky. Their role is to provide landmarks in a perspective representation of space.

Figure 13.   Dirk Bouts, *The Last Supper* (1464–1467), 6 feet high, Church of St. Peter, Louvain, Belgium. Photo: Charles Boils.

Bouts' finest painting is his great *Last Supper* (Louvain, Fig. 13), a triptych in the Church of St. Peter, Louvain, commissioned in 1464 by the Brotherhood of the Holy Sacrament and finished in 1467. The painting represents the solemn moment of the Institution of the Eucharist. The Eucharist theme is carried out in all four side panels, where Old Testament scenes prefigure the New Testament. The central panel of the *Last Supper* illustrates Bouts' interest in axial linear perspective. The head of Christ, His hand, the Wafer, and a series of vanishing points are all on the same line down the center of the panel; thus,

Bouts approached the one-point perspective of the Italian Renaissance. Bouts used a strong side light to heighten the tangibility of the forms. His color scheme was typical of the north, principally red, gray, and green. In the meeting of Abraham and Melchisedec, Bouts achieved a coherent representation of space with winding road and a panoramic landscape. As often happens in his paintings, the figures seem to be an afterthought; he had no interest in them except as forms to further define the progression of the space into the distance. Even miracles such as Elisha and the Angel are represented as completely normal occurrences. The Passover, another prototype of the Last Supper, was used by Bouts to demonstrate his skill in the representation of interior space at the same time he painted the yard of the inn outside.

Dirk Bouts painted the first portrait with a landscape view out the window, as well as the first Madonna with a landscape. Poses of the figures were borrowed from Roger van der Weyden; the lighting and interest in surfaces, from Jan van Eyck. From Christus, Bouts learned the definite interior setting, but he opened the window to a view, creating a unity of interior and exterior. In his interest in landscape and group portraits, Dirk Bouts anticipated seventeenth-century Flemish painting.

Geertgen tot Sint Jans (*ca.* 1460–*ca.* 1490), a young artist working in Haarlem in the 1480's, produced many paintings before his early death at the age of 28. He was a mystic, following the practical mysticism expounded by the Brotherhood of the Common Life. Just as this teaching order translated the Bible into the vernacular, so did Geertgen translate religious subjects into scenes from everyday life. Geertgen's paintings have a naive, youthful character and a natural, simple feeling. Nevertheless, his work was progressive, for he attempted to unify the elements of space, light, and color. Geertgen's masterpiece is the *Holy Kinship* (Amsterdam, *ca.* 1480, Fig. 14). The Madonna and Child with all their relatives are seated in a Romanesque church, perhaps a reference to their Old Testament inheritance. Christ's sacrifice and the salvation of man are prefigured in the decoration of the choir and altar of the church. While the composition and architectural setting of the painting were based on earlier artists' work, the conception of the figures was Geertgen's own. The figures are at once flat patterns and simple, round objects created by strong light and dark contrasts.

The followers of Roger van der Weyden emphasized the gentle beauty and the decorative quality of his painting. They developed a style of great refinement known as the *détente* or "relaxed" style. The principal exponent of the *détente* was Hans Memling (*ca.* 1435–1494). Memling was born near Frankfurt and was probably influenced in his youth by the School of Cologne (Chapter 4). He was Roger van der

Figure 14. Geertgen tot Sint Jans, *The Holy Kinship* (ca. 1480), 54 × 41½", Rijksmuseum, Amsterdam, The Netherlands.

Weyden's assistant in Brussels and finished the donor portraits on the Columba Altarpiece. After Van der Weyden's death, he moved to Bruges where by 1470 he was listed as one of the hundred wealthy citizens. Memling's style is characterized by simplicity, harmony, and refinement. He combined Van Eyck's settings with Van der Weyden's figure types and, after about 1485, added some Italian Renaissance ornament and architectural details. His color harmony resembles that of Fra Angelico, powdery and tempera-like with much gold. His favorite themes were incidents in lives of female Saints and the Madonna and Child with Angels, symmetrical compositions with a quiet, vertical balance.

One of Memling's most characteristic and delightful works is the *Shrine of St. Ursula* (Bruges, 1489, Fig. 15), a Gothic reliquary with a lively depiction of the story of St. Ursula and her ten thousand companions. Flemish realism appears in the representation of actual buildings, such as Cologne Cathedral and the Lateran Baptistry. A very obviously idealized type of feminine beauty was created by Memling and was used throughout his work. Memling's flowing linear style set off the decorative qualities of the hair and garments of the figures against an ideal landscape. Brilliant colors and delicate drawing replaced religious intensity. The figures of saints are so aristocratic that even the martyrdom is rather elegant. Memling was also a very popular portrait painter, for his portraits were invariably flattering. The sitters are relaxed, elegant people placed in a loggia setting against a gentle landscape.

By the end of the fifteenth century, the old centers of culture were losing their wealth, and Antwerp developed as the new center of art. Typical of the artists who moved to Antwerp was Gerard David

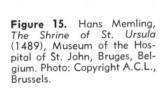

Figure 15. Hans Memling, *The Shrine of St. Ursula* (1489), Museum of the Hospital of St. John, Bruges, Belgium. Photo: Copyright A.C.L., Brussels.

(died 1523), a master of the *détente*. He may have been a pupil of Geertgen tot Sint Jans, but in 1484, he was mentioned in Bruges where he worked as a miniaturist before moving to Antwerp about 1515. Though an eclectic painter, he was still original in his interest in space, symmetry, and monumentality. His figures and settings are idealized and simplified. The paintings are characterized by solemn, slightly monotonous groups of symmetrical, statue-like figures. *The Rest on the Flight into Egypt* (Washington, D. C.) in the National Gallery is one of his most charming paintings.

THE INNOVATORS AT THE END OF THE CENTURY: HUGO VAN DER GOES AND HIERONYMOUS BOSCH

Perhaps the greatest painter of the late fifteenth century was Hugo van der Goes (*ca.* 1435–1482). The first date recorded for this artist is

1467 when he became a master of the painters' guild in Ghent. By 1474, he was dean of the painters' guild; however, in the next year he entered the Rhode Cloister near Brussels as a privileged lay brother suffering from depression and a belief in his own damnation. In 1481, a suicidal mania, described in a diary of Brother Gaspard of Tournai, siezed him and his case was diagnosed as insanity resulting from conscientiousness and overwork. He died the following year. Hugo's ambition seems to have been to combine the two-dimensional, linear composition, and expressive, emotional quality of Roger van der Weyden with the realistic detail and clear representation of space of Jan van Eyck. The intensity of his effort to achieve this new synthesis may have cost him his life.

One of his earliest paintings, the *Fall and Redemption of Man* (Vienna, 1467–1468, Fig. 16), although small in scale, was a more ambitious drama than had been attempted before. From the Ghent Altarpiece, he borrowed figure types and poses, the foreground landscape, and the lighting. Van der Goes, however, interpreted the Fall of Man with a new emphasis on guilt. As he visualized the event, Eve

Figure 16. Hugo van der Goes, *Adam and Eve* (one panel from the diptych, *Fall and Redemption of Man*) (1467–1468), Kunsthistorisches Museum, Vienna, Austria.

Figure 17. Hugo van der Goes, The Portinari Altarpiece (ca. 1476), center 8'3½" × 10', wings 8'3½" × 4'7½", Uffizi, Florence, Italy. Photo: Alinari–Art Reference Bureau.

had already bitten into the apple; thus, the Fall had already occurred. The role of Eve was emphasized by placing her in the center of the composition, a place usually held by the serpent. The diagonal line of the three heads was repeated in the diagonal movement of the landscape into space, adding to the sense of continuity between figures and the landscape. Van der Goes combined an incredibly accurate observation with a romantic feeling for light and the representation of nature. The companion panel, the *Lamentation*, is related to the painting of Robert Campin and Roger van der Weyden. Again, the painting is disturbingly melodramatic since the body of Christ was represented as still being lowered from the cross. An overly intense light, low and seemingly from behind the viewer, was contrasted with a cloudy sky, creating an indefinite background and a complex pattern of darks and reflected lights.

Hugo van der Goes' expressionistic style culminated in his only documented painting, the Portinari Altarpiece (Florence, *ca.* 1476, Fig. 17). The altarpiece was commissioned by Tomaso Portinari, the representative of the Medici in Bruges, and his wife, Maria Baroncelli, to be placed in the Baroncelli Chapel in Santa Maria Novella in Florence. The large scale, approximately 8½ by 19½ feet, may have been intended to rival the Florentine murals. The painting caused great excitement in Italy on its arrival and was copied and studied for its representation of landscape and light by Italian artists such as Ghirlandaio, Filippo Lippi, and Piero de Cosimo. The three separate panels form a unified composition in which large figures move easily and naturally in a spacious setting. The Portinari Altarpiece has on the exterior the Annunciation and on the interior the Adoration of the Shepherds. In the wings are the donors with their patron saints. Behind Tomaso and his sons, Joseph and Mary travel painfully to Bethlehem; behind Maria and her daughter, the three Magi have lost their way and ask directions from a peasant. These themes of the swooning Mary and the lost Magi are disturbingly emotional. Van der Goes was concerned with the total man, with the psychological as well as the physical state of the individual. The contrast in scale between the looming patron saints, the kneeling donors, and the tiny background figures is disconcerting. Even the landscape, whitened to the horizon with a cold light, carries an emotional impact.

Representation of the Adoration of the Shepherds in the center panel is based on St. Bridget's visions of the Madonna and Child of Humility. In keeping with the extremes of emotion the artist hoped to induce, extremes in subject matter and representation were used; for example, the elegance, delicacy, and richness of the angels is contrasted to the coarseness and poverty of the peasants and the humbleness of the Holy Family. The shepherds are some of the most striking examples of accurate observation in fifteenth-century art, although their representation is not yet wholly sympathetic. Van der Goes overemphasized, if anything, their earthiness. The composition recalls Van der Weyden's scheme of combining surface patterns and an underlying three-dimensional structure. Balance was achieved through diagonal axes intersecting at the center with the Madonna. Then, throughout the great work, Hugo combined a detailed rendering in subtle lights and patterns in the manner of Jan van Eyck with the monumentality and simplicity of Roger van der Weyden. Thus, the representation of maximum depth and, at the same time, the maximum surface detail added to the tension of the subject matter.

Van der Goes' personal conflict may be sensed throughout his work and especially in the paintings of his last years. These show both the grandeur of his style and his emotional intensity. *The Death of the Virgin* (Bruges, Fig. 18), Van der Goes' last painting, is a very unusual composition, a square eight feet high. A sixteenth-century drawing shows it crowned with a triangular pediment, and it may have had wings as well. The subject is the miraculous appearance of Christ and the gathering of the Apostles at the Death of the Virgin. This miracle is depicted with sharp realism, although the space is inconsistently represented. The Apostles seem to be drawn as a complex two-dimensional surface pattern, and yet the bed with the Virgin is radically foreshortened and cuts obliquely through the space. This contrast and tension between two- and three-dimensional patterns recalls Mannerist painting of the sixteenth century, as do the dry, cool colors of red, blue, green, and olive brown.

Hieronymous Bosch (*ca.* 1450–1516) bridged the fifteenth and sixteenth centuries. He was at the same time a Medievalist, a Mannerist, and a unique individual. Little is known about his life except that he was born in s'Hertogenbosch in the Netherlands and was a member of the Confraternity of Our Lady. Discussion of Bosch's style has been obscured by the fascination of his subject matter. When he painted a well-known theme, he treated it unconventionally; even more often, he invented totally unconventional subjects. He delighted in physical and psychological monstrosities, and he observed the world and human nature with a keen eye and a vivid imagination. His grotesques, inspired by Gothic art, became very real. Some of his images can be found in northern literature, some in alchemy, and others were part of oral folk tradition.

Figure 18. Hugo van der Goes, *The Death of the Virgin* (*ca.* 1482), Groeningemuseum, Bruges, Belgium. Photo: Copyright A.C.L., Brussels.

The *Haywain* triptych (Madrid, Fig. 19) is Bosch's comment on the damnation of man whose life, he seemed to say, is one long road to hell. The center panel of the *Haywain* is a commentary on the Last Judgment with Christ represented as judge and Man of Sorrows and man's life is symbolized by a Flemish proverb—the world is a mountain of hay, and people commit the seven deadly sins to get more of it. The haywain is guided by devils and demons, and everyone, even popes and cardinals, chase after it in a mad frenzy. On top of the wagon, two wealthy couples are courting. Their guardian angel appeals to God, but a devil plays a tune, and the lovers ride along happily to hell. A continuous landscape unites Heaven, earth, and hell and seems to indicate that human history is only a stage on the road to hell.

The Garden of Earthly Delights (Madrid, *ca.* 1500, Fig. 20) is Bosch's masterpiece and his most rigorous statement of man's damnation. Again, a continuous landscape unites the three panels. Of the many possible interpretations, most plausible is the suggestion that the painting represents man's appetite for earthly delights which keep him on the level of a beast. Man sinned directly after creation and, thus, drove himself to hell. In the Garden of Eden, represented as a tropical landscape of hybrid plants and rocks filled with strange creatures, Eve

Figure 19. Hieronymus Bosch, *The Haywain* (center panel) (*ca.* 1500), The Prado, Madrid, Spain. Photo: Mas.

Figure 20. Hieronymus Bosch, *The Garden of Earthly Delights* (center panel) (*ca.* 1500), 86½ × 76¾'', The Prado, Madrid, Spain. Photo: Mas.

is just coming to life while Adam watches astonished. Sin and lust already existed in Bosch's Eden, and lust rather than curiosity was responsible in his depiction of the Fall of Man. The Fountain of Life, formed of egg shapes and spiney stems and housing the owl of heresy, produced ponds which are spawning grounds for slimy, hybrid monsters. The descendents of Adam and Eve race wildly about in a light and pulsating landscape made up of fantastic mixtures of objects. The foreground is filled with a scene of sheer chaos, a perpetual Eve of St. Agnes, while in the middleground, maidens cavort in a pond around which prances a mad cavalry of men riding fantastic beasts. The carefully calculated structure of the painting may be forgotten by the spectator in his fascination with the monstrous and beautiful details.

Hell, as represented by Bosch, is an extreme of earthly desires, an upside down world in which pleasures have become pain. Bosch seems to say that, given freedom of choice, Adam and Eve literally drove themselves out of Paradise, and ever since, the evils of the world have been man's own doing. In spite of the superficial Medievalism of his paintings, especially the highly imaginative quality, Bosch's belief in individual responsibility makes him a man of the Renaissance.

Although Bosch used the fifteenth-century technique of sharp outlines and glazes of clear thinly applied paint, and his cool colors have tremendous decorative charm, his world seems far from that of his fifteenth-century contemporaries. Bosch was not interested in the human figure as such. He valued man only as an expressive vehicle for his imagination. Landscape was his delight. Bosch, like twentieth-century artists, used a shifting viewpoint, representing landscape from above and the figures from the side or even from below. He also contrasted surface interest with deep plunges into space. This curious dualism in space is one of the fascinations of Bosch's paintings, and it became an important aspect of the Mannerist style in the sixteenth century.

4

Fifteenth-Century Painting Outside Flanders

During the fifteenth century, the style and technique developed in the Low Countries spread throughout Europe. Wherever Flemish artists travelled or their paintings were carried, the local artists adopted their luminous colors and microscopic realism. The more intricate religious symbolism and the profound study of man and his environment were less often mastered. When representing human beings, the artists outside Flanders learned to record man's physical appearance but only rarely, and almost accidentally, did they suggest his personality. In painting landscape, the artists tended to concentrate on details of nature in a way reminiscent of the International Style. The study of space and light and the organization of the visual world into a coherent composition were not the artists' major concerns. Thus, the fifteenth-century artists of Germany, France, or Spain retained many of the elements found in their local version of the Late Gothic style in their adaptation of the Flemish style.

GERMAN, AUSTRIAN, AND SWISS PAINTING

German, Austrian, or Swiss artists differed from the Flemish in their greater concern for the emotional impact of their subjects. Their paintings were characterized by expressive linearity, abstract color, a disregard of spatial relationships, and a delight in direct, emphatic narration. The Gothic point of view persisted, especially along the Rhine where the mysticism of the churchmen influenced the painters. In contrast to the positive, active mystics in the Netherlands, the German mystics advocated the renunciation of reason and the dependence on pure feeling and subjective personal experience in an attempt to unite the soul with God. This attitude toward life was best expressed in the Cologne School of painting, of which Stefan Lochner (1405–1451) was the leading exponent. Lochner created a timeless world peopled by gentle figures floating in a golden space. His *Madonna of the Rose Garden* (Cologne, Fig. 21) represented the mystics' eternal adoration of the Madonna and Child. The serene world of Heaven was represented as a rose arbor against a golden sky. Mary sits, seeing nothing, doing nothing, the epitome of renunciation of personal will. Lochner aimed for perfect harmony by limiting his colors as much as possible to the primary hues and by placing his forms symmetrically in the simplest possible composition.

Conrad Witz (1400/10–1444/46), the most remarkable individual personality in German fifteenth-century painting, established the style for the upper Rhine. He was born in Rottweile and was working in Basel by 1434. Both his direct approach to the visual world and the sculpturesque quality of his figures make him unique, although his sources can be found in the work of Robert Campin and Jan van Eyck. Witz's Altarpiece of St. Peter (Geneva, signed and dated 1444, Fig. 22) illustrates his interest in space. In the *Miraculous Draught of the Fishes,* he created the first topographically accurate landscape in northern art. He established a broad foreground plane in which the figures and the architecture were carefully placed to lead the viewer

Figure 21. Stefan Lochner, *Madonna of the Rose Garden* (ca. 1440), 20 × 16", Wallraf - Richartz Museum, Cologne, Germany. Photo: Rheinisches Bildarchiv.

Figure 22. Conrad Witz, *The Miraculous Draught of the Fishes* (1444), 51 × 61", Musée d'art et d'histoire, Geneva, Switzerland.

across the sea to the opposite shore, the city of Geneva, and Mont Blanc. This progression into far distance was achieved by converting the landscape into a series of carefully structured cubical forms, and then uniting it all with a gleaming, sweeping light. While the landscape was inspired by Van Eyck and his followers, the figures are reminiscent of Campin in their vigor and massiveness.

A leading painter of the Black Forest region was Lucas Moser. In his Mary Magdalene Altarpiece (Tiefenbronn, signed and dated 1431), the figures at first seem to be mere splashes of color to which a rich surface pattern was added and then juxtaposed with a gold background. Under Flemish influence, he attempted some realistic space relationships. Although he was a cruder and bolder painter, Lucas Moser seems to have been influenced by Robert Campin whose style spread as far as the Lake Constance region. Moser's famous lament, "Weep, o art, your fate deplore, no one loves you anymore," probably referred to his fellow artists' new concern with the visible world rather than "art."

In southern Germany, Michael Pacher (*ca.* 1435–1498) of Salzburg and Michael Wolgemut (1434–1519) of Nuremburg were the leading artists. Pacher's Altarpiece of the Four Latin Fathers (Munich) is a magnificent Late Gothic combination of painting and sculpture. Pacher evidently knew Italian Renaissance painting, for his own work was influenced by the Italian development of linear perspective; however, his figures are typically northern in style. Wolgemut based his work entirely on Flemish models. From 1470 to 1500, he had a flourishing workshop in Nuremburg where he was the teacher of Albrecht Dürer.

GERMAN GRAPHIC ARTS

Development of the graphic arts during the fifteenth century is one of the most significant contributions of northern Europe to the history of art. Although the specific origins of the woodcut are unknown, artists in the Rhineland and northern France first exploited the medium. The earliest woodcuts (about 1400 to 1430) were religious images produced to satisfy the desire of the common man to own a sacred image. For example, in the painting of the *Annunciation* by Robert Campin, a woodcut of St. Christopher is fastened above the fireplace. These early prints are characterized by very heavy lines, lack of shading, and first round and later angular patterns. They were usually hand colored. One of the most famous early prints is a *Saint Christopher* from southern Germany, dated 1423. Saint Christopher was the patron saint of travellers, and prints were produced for sale to pilgrims as protection. The reduction of the scene to a two-dimensional pattern is in keeping with the dematerialized art of the fourteenth century rather than the spatial investigation of the fifteenth. *Saint Christopher* seems to be based on a miniature painting and something of the painters' vivid narration and three-dimensional quality remains.

About 1450, the block book, in which the text and illustrations were cut on a single block, was invented. The book differed from manuscripts in its elimination of detail, rather rough style, and naive folk quality. Color was still usually added by hand after the printing. The *Ars Moriendi*, or art of dying, was a popular fourteenth- and fifteenth-century theme. The earliest printed copy, *ca.* 1450–1460, reflected the sophisticated style of the Van Eycks. The most popular of all the block books was the *Biblia Pauperum*. The script followed the manuscript tradition, while the illustrations were made from separate blocks with an added block as a decorative frame. The style was angular; however, the figures were active and placed in a definite setting. In the *Legends of the Saints* from Augsburg (1474), the pages are single decorative units with the type and illustration designed together. Tonal qualities were achieved by hatching which replaced hand coloring. These books, which gave the individual a greater opportunity for religious study without the established church as intermediary, formed a basis for the Protestant Reformation.

Engraving developed a little later than the woodcut, partly in emulation of the older medium. The engravings were finer prints than the woodcuts. Since the engravers belonged to the goldsmiths' guild, they were of a higher class than the woodcut masters and aimed for the patronage of an elite social group. Their technique was much more delicate, more subtle; the prints were more intimate. The early engravers were slow to learn to make curves in the shading; thus, the contours of a form were often curvilinear but the interior lines were all straight; single parallel lines rather than cross-hatching were used for shading. The style was simple, and at the same time more monumental and subtle than woodcut.

The Master of the Playing Cards (active 1430–1445) is the earliest important engraver. His style was influenced by the art of Conrad Witz. His figures were rather heavy, as was characteristic of the art of southern Germany; an interest in natural detail was subordinated to the overall theme, and the composition was built up with rhythmic, swinging lines.

During the second half of the fifteenth century, engraving lost its naive, folk quality. Master E.S. (active 1440/50–1467), a German-Swiss from the upper Rhine, was the finest artist of the period. His style is closely related to the sculpture from the area of Frankfurt, and his concern for detail and ornament indicates that he was trained as a goldsmith. His early works show a mastery of the medium and an interest in a rich profusion of specific detail. Draperies were represented by strongly breaking angular folds whose textures are suggested with considerable skill by means of cross-hatching to give luminosity to the darks. Later, he learned to subordinate the masses of natural details in his extensive backgrounds, and he produced monumental, coherent designs.

Martin Schongauer (*ca.* 1430–1491) was the last of the Medieval and the first of the Renaissance graphic artists. He lived in Colmar, and although he attended the University of Leipzig, he was trained as a goldsmith and painter and may have studied with the Master E.S. at Strassbourg. Schongauer was conscious of his individuality as an artist, for he signed his prints. He had a better understanding of space than the Master E.S. although he avoided the problems of the middleground by setting the figure on a cliff and letting the background fall away from it. There is a more pictorial variation in his use of black and white, and a greater concentration and power in his prints. He modelled surfaces, especially fabrics, in a less abstract way, and he seemed to have a real understanding of the movements of drapery over a figure. He was a great graphic artist, technically so skillful that he was able to capture an emotion even while he schematized forms. Characteristic of his work is the *Temptation of St. Anthony,* an engraving which even Michelangelo admired. The visionary quality of Schongauer's prints appeal to the imagination even though the Late Gothic demons are now more decorative than frightening. The print is a Gothic fantasy of restless crowded details, curving surfaces, elongated figures, exaggerated joints, long tubular folds, masses of small S-curves.

Schongauer's finest late work is the *Madonna in a Courtyard* (Fig. 23). Here, the complexity of the Medieval style is gone and the simplicity of the Renaissance appears. The artist aimed for an ideal, universal type. The cubic solidity and the monumentality of the figure emphasize its primary importance, and the walls and tower concentrate the viewer's attention on the Madonna. The linear patterns of the bare tree and

Figure 23. Martin Schongauer, *Madonna in a Courtyard* (ca. 1480), courtesy, Museum of Fine Arts, Boston, Harvey D. Parker Collection.

the decorative curling locks of Mary's hair contrast with the severity of the composition as a whole.

Schongauer's skill as an engraver surpassed his talents as a painter. The *Madonna and Child* in Colmar shows him to be precise and linear as a draftsman, but weak as a colorist.

The drypoint technique was developed by the Housebook Master, also known as the Master of the Amsterdam Cabinet. He was probably a German working near Frankfurt in the last quarter of the fifteenth century. Drypoint allows the artist more freedom since the drawing is done directly on relatively soft metals such as lead. The Housebook Master's style is remarkably vigorous. He draws with many scratchy, irregular lines, creating a diffused quality of the outline which helps to achieve an atmospheric effect. His best prints have the freedom of pen and ink drawings. He is perplexingly original in his naturalism and his humor and in the genre touches which depart radically from traditional iconography.

With the work of Schongauer and the Housebook Master, the basis has been laid for the brilliant culmination of the graphic arts in the work of Albrecht Dürer.

FRENCH PAINTING

French painting of the fifteenth century lacked the unity of accomplishment seen elsewhere in Europe. The country had been devastated by the Hundred Years War, recovery was slow, and no city could support a group of painters. In both France and England, painting was still considered a minor art and available funds were used for buildings. French painting of the fifteenth century was characterized by rather mundane realism combined with carefully controlled surface patterns which gave the final product a curious quality of reserve, aloofness, and courtly elegance. These characteristics are even apparent in religious paintings such as the *Avignon Pietà* (Paris, *ca.* 1490). The artist used arbitrary colors and a gold background which conflict with the broad and deep landscape vista. Monumental forms and inexpressive faces were contrasted with the intense emotional significance of the painting as a whole. An awareness of everyday life and human suffering seems an intrusion on the formal, two-dimensional composition.

Jean Fouquet (*ca.* 1425–*ca.* 1485) was the finest and most typical French fifteenth-century painter. Although he directed a large manuscript workshop in Tours, he is best known for his portraits. These portraits were not commanding psychological studies. Instead, the formal decorative aspects of costume and setting were emphasized in almost shocking contrast to the mundane realism of the faces. In the portrait of *Etienne Chevalier* with his patron St. Stephen (Berlin, *ca.* 1455, Fig. 24), Fouquet reached the height of his powers. While the color is striking and the composition is daring, the technique as a whole is conservative. The firm contours and the sense of pattern are reminiscent of Piero della Francesco, and the architectural setting is filled with Italian decorative motifs which Fouquet learned on a trip to Italy about 1447. These superficial Renaissance details represent the first penetration of the Italian fifteenth-century style into France.

Figure 24. Jean Fouquet, *Etienne Chevalier and St. Stephen* (ca. 1455), 36½ × 33½", State Museums, Berlin, Germany.

SPANISH PAINTING

Painting at the beginning of the fifteenth century in Spain was still Gothic in character and emphasized magnificent decorative effects and crisp silhouettes. Typically Spanish was an extensive use of gold, the lavish embossing of the halos, crowns, embroidered garments or armor, heaviness of the decoration in general, and elaborate costumes. The International Style artists' enthusiasm for nature without knowledge of its underlying structure was continued in tapestry-like panoramic landscapes filled with fantastic hills, plants, and animals. Bernardo Martorell (active 1427–1452), the leading Catalan painter during the early fifteenth century, is typical of this phase of Spanish painting. His *St. George and the Dragon* (Chicago, 1430, Fig. 25) is still essentially an unrealistic painting where the minute detail is based on preconceptions rather than direct visual experience. Martorell was a master of the fluid, curving line and miniature-like colors. He occasionally used embossed gold backgrounds, contrasting with his tentative suggestion of foreground space.

During the second half of the fifteenth century, direct contact with Flemish art led to the development of a Hispano-Flemish style. Not only were Flemish paintings brought to Spain but Spanish artists studied the Flemish style and technique firsthand. Luis Dalmau (active 1428–1460) travelled in the Netherlands in 1431 where he must have seen the Ghent Altarpiece. The influence of Van Eyck's masterpiece is strong in Dalmau's monumental painting, the *Madonna of the Councilors of*

Figure 25. Bernardo Martorell, *St. George and the Dragon* (1430), 56 × 38", courtesy of the Art Institute of Chicago, Illinois.

Barcelona (Barcelona, 1445, Fig. 26). Figures, portraits, architectural settings, and landscapes are all based on the Van Eycks' style, and specific details such as the singing angels, distant cities, and the bearded saint are almost literal copies from the inner panels of the Ghent Altarpiece.

Bartolomé Bermejo (1440–1489) also may have studied in the north for his technique is completely Flemish. *Santa Engracia* (Boston) is very close to the Van Eycks in the drawing and the enamel-like surface

Figure 26. Luis Dalmau, *Madonna of the Councilors of Barcelona* (1445), Museum of Catalan Art, Barcelona, Spain. Photo: Mas.

of strong, pure colors. The distinctive Spanish character of the painting lies in superficial matters such as the costume, the Spanish facial type, and the use of the Moorish eight-pointed star in the floor patterns. Three-dimensional space is hardly suggested. The throne behind the saint provides a decorative frame for the figure and creates no sense of depth, and the tilted floor forms a flat pattern against the gold background.

On the other hand, the *Pietà* with a donor and St. Jerome (Barcelona, signed and dated 1490, Fig. 27) shows a radical change at the end of Bermejo's life, following a trip to Italy about 1485. In this work, he painted a broad, generalized landscape which recalls Italian art with a Flemish donor portrait and Spanish drapery. The seriousness to the point of morbidity, the terrible physical destruction of Christ and the emphasis on the Passion and suffering are characteristic of Spanish art.

In the painting of Pedro Berruguete (*ca.* 1450–1504), the transition was made to the Renaissance in Spain. Berruguete spent five years (1477–1482) at the Court of Urbino working with Justus von Ghent and Piero della Francesco on decorations for the palace of the Duke Federico. By 1483, he was back in Spain and is traceable there until

Figure 27. Bartolomé Bermejo, *Pietà* (1490), Cathedral Museum, Barcelona, Spain. Photo: Mas.

his death. Particularly interesting is his version of the *Beheading of John the Baptist* (Sta. María del Campo, 1483, Fig. 28) where the influence of Urbino may be seen in such details as the Renaissance door with classical pilasters and Federico's monogram, FCDX, on the lintel. Italian, too, is the one-point linear perspective defined by the tile floor and open door as well as the scientific interest in anatomy and movement. These Italian features in Berruguete's work lessened with time. On the high altar of Santo Tomás in Avila (1490–1495), Berruguete returned to a more typically Spanish style. He consciously reduced the appearance of space to create a decorative, two-dimensional design which he then contrasted with a serious, almost grim, mood.

ENGLISH PAINTING

England during the fifteenth century had neither the material resources nor the security necessary for the patronage of painting. The country had not recovered from the last waves of the plague at the

Figure 28. Pedro Berruguete, *Beheading of John the Baptist* (1483), Sta. María del Campo, Spain. Photo: Mas.

end of the fourteenth century nor from the Hundred Years War, when the disastrous War of the Roses broke out. The native tradition of English painting, which had flourished from the Anglo-Saxon period, was broken. Some retables and a few paintings on walls of churches have survived; however, the treatment of subjects was anecdotal and the execution was poor. A frequent and popular theme was the three living and the three dead kings, probably copied from manuscripts or, later, from prints.

5

Sculpture and Architecture
in the Fifteenth Century

Sculpture and architecture during the fifteenth century were profoundly influenced by painting. The painters' concern with the visible world led to experiments with space, light, and movement as well as with attempts to depict man and nature realistically. The sculptors, in turn, began to think of their figures as free beings in an earthly, spatial environment rather than as architectural members. Under the leadership of Claus Sluter in Burgundy, they developed a style concentrating on visual effects which would later come to be known as a "painterly" representation of forms. In architecture, the Medieval building practices were continued; however, the structural forms were aesthetically dematerialized as architects, too, concentrated on effects of light and movement. Masons and carpenters defied the technical limitations of their art in the creation of continuous flowing movements and interpenetrating spaces and forms.

FRENCH SCULPTURE

A new style of sculpture was created at the end of the fourteenth century by Claus Sluter (ca. 1360–1406), who worked for Philip the Bold of Burgundy. Sluter was born in southern Holland and joined the workshop of Jean de Marville in Dijon, Burgundy, about 1384. The shop was employed by Philip to build the Carthusian monastery of Champmol as a pantheon for the Ducal house. By the end of the fourteenth century, Sluter was the director of the shop. The portal of the Chapel (1385–1393, Fig. 29) was based on the typical Gothic composition with jamb and trumeau figures; however, the architecture no longer dominated the sculpture but acted as a backdrop in which bases and canopies were expanded to form a stage space for independent figures. In the jambs, the two donors kneel with their patrons, Philip the Bold with St. John the Baptist and Margaret with St. Catherine, focusing their attention on the Madonna and Child on the trumeau. In Sluter's style, the visual effect transcends the individual architectural and sculptural elements. Elaborate, deeply cut forms and vigorous movements resulted in a play of light and shade over the surface of the sculpture. The voluminous draperies, arranged in horizontal folds, hint at bodies with bulk and substance beneath. The sculptors, like the painters, excelled in realistic surface details. The face of the Duke is a masterpiece of portraiture. The effectiveness of the sculpture, in realistic terms, must have been enhanced by equally natural polychrome.

Figure 29. Claus Sluter, Portal of the Carthusian Monastery of Champmol (1385–1393), Dijon, France. Photo: ND Giraudon.

Sluter's masterpiece, carved for the cloister of the monastery, was the *Well of Moses* (1395–1406, Fig. 30). The *Well of Moses* takes its name from the column placed in the center of the well and decorated with Old Testament prophets who foretold the coming of Christ and His Passion, prophecies which were fulfilled by the Crucifixion and for which the column provided a structural as well as symbolic base. Sluter's well was a symbol of the Baptism, the Eucharist, and the source of the Rivers of Paradise. The pedestal with prophets survives in place, and fragments of the Crucifixion are now in the Archaeological Museum in Dijon. The massiveness and volumetric quality of the figures

Figure 30. Claus Sluter, *The Well of Moses* (1395–1406), height of figures 5'8", Carthusian Monastery of Champmol, Dijon, France. Photo: Estel—Blois.

was achieved through a new sense of light and pictorial organization. The sculpture was originally painted to increase this illusionistic quality. Gestures and facial expressions were used to bring out the character of each figure. The realism of the prophets, alternating between vigorous and weary figures, suggests that Claus Sluter may have used living models for his sculpture. The most famous of the figures is the ancient, angry Moses. So realistically represented is he that even his "horns" are wrinkled. Like his Gothic predecessors, Sluter was interested in the gestures and expressions of hands and faces and in the patterns made by the fall of elaborate, heavy drapery, but not by the human figure alone.

Sluter exerted a powerful influence on the artists of his day, and his style dominated northern sculpture for the next hundred years. Not only was French sculpture of the fifteenth century dependent on the work of Claus Sluter for its most powerful statements, but Flanders, Spain, and Germany were all more or less influenced by him.

In areas where Sluter's influence was not strong, French sculpture retained all the idealism of the High Gothic but little of its monumentality. Force and grandeur gave way to gentle beauty. Graceful figures, at once Medieval and Renaissance, adorn the churches in cities such as Troyes. The finest sculpture at the end of the century was the Tomb of Francis II of Brittany (1502) in the Cathedral of Nantes attributed to Michel Colombe (1473–1512/1519). This style is known as the *détente,* and it expressed a similar mood in sculpture to that found in the painting of Hans Memling.

SPANISH SCULPTURE

Early fifteenth-century sculpture in Spain was closely related to France. Sculptors showed an early interest in realism, yet their work was essentially decorative in conception. At first, the artists were inspired by the full, luxuriant forms used by French thirteenth-century carvers at the Cathedral of Reims. Later, the deeper carving of forms and emphasis on light and shade effects were based on a knowledge of the work of Claus Sluter. The broad, massive draperies in curving rhythmic horizontal folds, the feeling for materials, the strength and power of the figure were characteristics brought into Spain by Burgundian artists who taught the new style to the Spaniards.

Spain's leading sculptor in the second half of the fifteenth century was Gil de Siloe (active in Spain 1447–1499). He may have originally come from France, and he was active in Burgos at the end of the fifteenth century where he carved the double Tomb of John II and

Isabel of Portugal (1486, 1489–1493, Fig. 31), the wall Tomb of Prince Alonso (1489–1494), and the High Altar in the Carthusian monastery of Miraflores (1496–1499, Fig. 32). The free standing tomb of the king and queen at the foot of the altar has the shape of an eight-pointed star lavishly carved with plants, animals, and figures of saints. The effigies are turned slightly to the side in order to be visible to the spectator, and they are framed in niches with rich architectural canopies. Their draperies are arranged as though the figures were standing. The virtuosity of the carving is seen in the realistic representation of the minutest details, for example, the carving of the lace, the jewels, and the brocades of the garments; however, these effects of realism are achieved without knowledge of the human body although there is a great vitality and energy in the sculpture as a whole.

The High Altar at Miraflores was designed by Gil de Siloe and carried out by his workshop. The gilded and painted wooden structure rises the full height of the building. The design is based on repeated circles, the largest of which encloses the Passion. This repetition of one geometric shape is a typically Islamic device. In the Spanish altarpieces (or *retablos*), the artists strove for a general effect rather than

Figure 31. Gil de Siloe, Tomb of John II and Isabel of Portugal (1486, 1489 – 1493), Carthusian Monastery of Miraflores, Burgos, Spain. Photo: Mas.

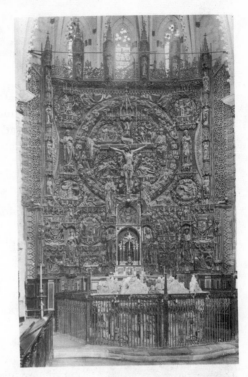

Figure 32. Gil de Siloe and assistants, *High Altar* (1496–1499), Carthusian Monastery of Miraflores, Burgos, Spain. Photo: Mas (Tomb of John II and Isabel in foreground).

the perfection of individual details, although the details are strongly realistic. Small stage-like settings show Flemish influence, but the enormous size, filling the entire east end of the church, is characteristically Spanish.

GERMAN AND NETHERLANDISH SCULPTURE

Love of rich detail and an interest in realism were also typical of German fifteenth-century sculpture. However, whereas the Spanish artist emphasized the decorative possibilities of his forms, the German tried to create an emotional identification with the subject on the part of the beholder. The greatest sculptors of the late fifteenth and early sixteenth centuries in Germany were Tilman Riemenschneider (*ca.* 1460–1531) and Viet Stoss (active 1477–1533). By combining a dynamic linearism with grace and adding both to the usual German extreme of realism and emotionalism, Riemenschneider achieved a new form of emotional religious expression. One of his favorite themes is the Madonna and Child, a fine example of which is in the collection of the University of

Figure 33. Tilman Riemenschneider, *Madonna and Child* (1490's), 47½ inches high, courtesy of University of Kansas Museum of Art, Lawrence, Kansas.

Kansas (1490's, Fig. 33). Here, he combined his love of intricate spatial relations, moving light and shade patterns, decorative draperies, realistic detail with a sweetness and tenderness of mood reminiscent of the *détente*. Riemenschneider usually placed his figures in a frame of fanciful architecture in which space and form are completely interpenetrating.

The sculpture of Viet Stoss of Nuremburg is characterized by crisp, angular, decorative forms, hard individualism, and realistic detail. The spectacular quality of Stoss' wood carving is exemplified by the great *Annunciation* (1518, Fig. 38) hung in the choir of the Church of St. Lawrence in Nuremburg. Interpenetration of space and form and the creation of moving light and shadow are at their most effective in this sculpture which literally floats, an object of mystical contemplation and adoration, over the altar.

Sculpture in the Netherlands never held the place that painting did. The great innovations and the most effective statements of the fifteenth century were made by the painters. Sculptors, such as Jan Borremans (flourished 1479–1522), developed the "stage space" concept of the painters in their designs for large altarpieces composed of a series of boxes into which lively figures were crowded. Anecdotal realism was carried to the ultimate extreme with figures, settings, and costumes all copied from daily life. This genre quality of the sculpture was contrasted with the florid architectural settings. Pictorial effects were so stressed at the expense of architectural or sculptural values that the total work of art often lost its force. The intricacy, immediacy, and lively narration appealed to the public in northern Europe and Spain, and Flemish altarpieces were exported over the continent. Large workshops were established for the production of religious sculpture, tomb slabs, and ecclesiastical and domestic furniture.

ENGLISH SCULPTURE

English sculpture in the fifteenth century was limited to architectural decoration, tombs, and alabaster altarpieces. Tombs usually con-
sisted of an effigy, represented as though standing, lying on a sarcophagus
which was placed in a chapel, itself a small replica of a Perpendicular
building. The carving of the figures was oversimplified, with the hair
and garments used to create decorative rhythmic movements. Realistic
portraits were not attempted. Military effigies were especially frequent,
and the type was repeated for generations, the principal changes taking
place in the style of armor from chain mail to plate armor to extravagant
Italian parade costumes. The rich and jewel-like carving of earlier figures
disappeared and was replaced by bold, simplified cutting and a strong
sense of three-dimensional design.

Alabaster sculpture, particularly small altarpieces, became an English
specialty in the fifteenth century. These altars were made for export
and can still be found all over Europe. Compact scenes, based on
religious drama such as the York Mystery Plays, were represented with
great energy by stiff elongated figures. Again, once the style and
iconography was established, there was little change for over a hundred
years.

FRENCH ARCHITECTURE

Fifteenth-century architecture in France remained conservative, an
elaboration and variation on the Gothic style, although the architects'
interest in space and surface finish are evident. The Flamboyant Style
of the fifteenth century was characterized by curves and flame-like
shapes, as well as by a love of elegant decoration and, significantly,
a new interest in space. The Church of St. Maclou at Rouen (1434–1470,
Fig. 34) is one of the finest examples of this style. Its plan was that
of a Gothic parish church; however, the structural skeleton was at-
tenuated and reduced until the space seems to have eaten away the
solid forms. Larger forms were subdivided, achieving a lace-like effect;
the pointed arch was treated fantastically rather than functionally.
Structural forms were turned into decorative devices suspended in front
of the walls and requiring the liberal use of tie rods to achieve the
necessary architectural stability. The architect had, in effect, returned
to wall construction. Ultimately, the building is conceived of as a
mass; the façade is indeed a wall; and a "Gothic structure" is applied
as decoration in low relief.

Although religious architecture still set the pace in the fifteenth century, secular architecture became increasingly important. Houses, markets, guild halls, and civic buildings of all kinds attest to the wealth and power of the middle class throughout Europe. Civic pride and growing industrialism are symbolized by the towering height of belfries over the town halls of northern France and Belgium. The House of Jacques Couer in Bourges (1443–1451, Fig. 35) is a palatial illustration of the fifteenth-century domestic ideal. Rooms and staircases were grouped around a central courtyard creating a functional, asymmetrical arrangement. Steep roofs and numerous chimneys were designed for the northern climate. More modest buildings of similar style were constructed of timber and brick.

Figure 34. St. Maclou (1434–1470), Rouen, France. Photo: Ellebe.

Figure 35. Courtyard, House of Jacques Couer (1443–1451), Bourges, France. Photo: ND Giraudon.

SPANISH ARCHITECTURE

As mentioned previously, one of the richest and most powerful centers in Europe in the fifteenth century was Spain. Not only did building reach new heights of magnificence under the Catholic Kings but the style and techniques were carried to the Americas. Thus, the earliest colonial building in the New World was Spanish Late Gothic in form.

Seville was the Spanish port serving the "Indies," and one of the most imposing buildings of the fifteenth century is the Cathedral of Seville, built between 1401 and 1520. No precedent existed in Christian architecture for the rectangular plan of the Cathedral which was built on the site of the mosque and adhered to its form. The bell tower of the church, the famous *Giralda,* was originally the minaret of the mosque. Although the exterior of the Cathedral is now masked by sixteenth-century additions, the horizontal composition of the building is still apparent. Even the buttresses slope upward only slightly, and balustrades mask exposed vaults. In the interior, very high aisles help create the effect of an enormous unified space hardly broken by compound piers subdivided into many vertical shafts. The clerestory is relatively small, for the sun and heat make large expanses of glass less desirable here than in northern Europe. The Cathedral of Seville was an important

Figure 36. Juan Güas, Interior of St. John of the Kings (begun 1477), Toledo, Spain. Photo: Mas.

Figure 37. College of St. Gregory (1488–1496), Valladolid, Spain. Photo: Mas.

influence on later churches, for example, the Cathedrals of Salamanca and Segovia.

Perhaps even more important both as an original architectural composition and for its influence on later architecture was the Isabellan monastic or parish church, the finest of which is St. John of the Kings (Toledo, Fig. 36). This church was ordered from Juan Güas (active 1459–1496) by Ferdinand and Isabel in 1477 as a mausoleum. An Isabellan church, such as St. John's, is characterized by the use of a single nave with lateral chapels between the buttresses, a raised western choir, and Moorish star-shaped vaults. An octagonal lantern on squinches with lavish pinnacles and balustrades was placed over the sanctuary. The exterior of the building is severe; however, interior wall surfaces are covered with sculpture. Coats of arms and inscriptions used as decorative elements are distinctively Isabellan decorative features. The cloister of St. John of the Kings is one of the most elaborate in Europe. Figures of saints were placed on piers supporting a mixtilinear arcade whose elaborate cuspings and trefoils are characteristically Spanish. The mouldings are covered with delicate realistic carving in very high relief of plants, insects, animals, and birds, all resembling the painted borders of manuscripts.

The florid Spanish Gothic reaches its height in the façade of the College of St. Gregory in Valladolid (1488–1496, Fig. 37). The façade, designed as a gigantic sculptured altarpiece, seems to stand in front of the building rather than act as a part of it. Realism was carried to an extreme in which the shafts were carved to resemble bundles of twigs, the balustrade was designed as a rustic fence, and the walls were covered with imitation wattlework. The theme of the façade is the glorification of Isabel and Ferdinand, and their coat of arms forms the central motif for the sculpture. Heralds and "wild men" take the place of saints, and the religious figures are relegated to a small tympanum.

GERMAN ARCHITECTURE

The hall church was Germany's great contribution to Late Medieval architecture. Inside and out, the church was built as a single unified cubical entity. The aisles and nave were of the same height; there were no transepts; the aisles continued around the building to form the ambulatory; chapels were placed between the buttresses creating a continuous exterior wall. These buildings were lit by tall lancet windows in the aisles. The piers were tall, unbroken, and angular with the ribs of the net-like vault springing directly from them. The vault approached a barrel vault supported by the walls. The churches were once filled

Figure 38. Church of St. Lawrence (1445–1472), Nuremburg, Germany. Photo: Lagois (Viet Stoss, *Annunciation*, over the altar).

with elaborate wood carvings, forming movable ornamentation. The Church of St. Lawrence in Nuremburg (1445–1472, Fig. 38), where a choir in the hall church style was added to the basilican nave, is one of the finest examples of the form. Its wide bays, slender piers, and star vaults create one unified space. The tabernacle is placed asymmetrically at the left, and Viet Stoss' *Annunciation,* in wood, hangs in front of the altar, thus enhancing the quality of diagonally moving interior space.

ENGLISH ARCHITECTURE

Architecture flourished throughout the Middle Ages and Renaissance in England. A distinctively English style, known as the Perpendicular, was developed in which the builders strove for lower proportions, rectangular spaces, massive walls contrasting with large windows, and intricate surface decoration. Builders basing their techniques on Gothic masonry and carpentry were very imaginative and sophisticated. At Gloucester, in the cloister of the Cathedral (1351–1412), the fan vault which was to become a favorite of fifteenth-century master masons was developed. The fan vault may at first seem to be a purely decorative form; however, the "fans" are actually half-cones built like corbels in horizontal courses out from the wall. They, in turn, support the panels of a flat ceiling. The fan vault is, thus, hardly a vault at all, in the Gothic sense. Equally characteristic of Perpendicular architecture is the very fine carpentry seen in interior paneling and in magnificent hammerbeam or double hammerbeam ceilings.

One of the most characteristic building complexes, for which the Perpendicular proved admirably suited, was the university, and the oldest university buildings at Oxford and Cambridge are excellent examples of both the secular and religious architecture of the fifteenth century. Cloister-like quadrangles surrounded by assembly rooms, dormitories, libraries, and chapel illustrate the essentially functional character and the adaptability of the style. King's College Chapel, Cambridge (1446–1515, Figs. 39 and 40) was built by Reginald Ely (active 1438–1471) and John Wastell (active 1493–1515). The chapel is a large, rectangular hall, lighted by large windows and covered with an elaborate vault almost flat on the inside and masked by a parapet to emphasize its horizontality on the outside. Massive walls, lightened aesthetically by tracery or colonettes, contrast with the expanse of glass window. The opposition of vertical and horizontal lines and planes which gave the name to the style produced a building that was Renaissance in its regularity, its horizontality, and its massiveness. When Italian Renais-

Figure 39. Reginald Ely, King's College Chapel (1446–1515), Cambridge, England, courtesy of the Provost and Fellows of King's College, Cambridge. Photo: Edward Leigh.

sance architecture was introduced into the British Isles, the builders did not have to learn a whole new concept of space and form. They simply changed from Gothic to classical ornamental details.

Characteristic architectural and decorative forms developed in the fourteenth and fifteenth centuries persisted until the eighteenth century outside the centers of political and cultural life. Thus, the first houses and churches erected in North America are closer in style and building technique to the fifteenth century than to the Renaissance or Baroque

Figure 40. Reginald Ely, King's College Chapel (1446–1515), Cambridge, England, courtesy of the Provost and Fellows of King's College, Cambridge. Photo: Ramsey and Muspratt.

architecture of the European capitals. St. Luke's Church, Smithfield, Virginia, is a parish church in the north European style. The colonial homes of Massachusetts, with their half-timber frames, projecting second floors, small diamond paired windows, steeply pitched roofs, and massive chimneys are a provincial variation of English houses. Naturally, the European styles were modified by colonial artisans. The adaptation of European styles to American conditions is one of the interesting chapters in the cultural history of our country.

6

The Sixteenth Century

INTRODUCTION OF ITALIAN ART AND THEORY INTO EUROPE

Not until the sixteenth century did the Italian Renaissance make any appreciable impression on the rest of Europe, and even then it was so changed by the local artistic tradition that it often bore little resemblance to the art of the parent country. The sixteenth-century art of Flanders with its heritage from Jan van Eyck and Roger van der Weyden was quite unlike that of Spain, for example, where the Moors were only expelled in 1492.

Italian forms were introduced in a variety of ways and this, too, influenced the final expression of the style. Italian artists occasionally worked abroad; however, their influence was limited. More important in the spread of the style was the fact that native artists, on seeing Italian work or hearing of the new style, went to Italy to study, and, on their return, they introduced local artists to the new forms. Patrons of the arts travelled to Italy, especially the churchmen going to Rome and, on their return, tried to re-create something of the splendor they had seen in the Holy City. Finally, the Renaissance style was spread by books on art theory and, in architecture and architectural sculpture, by handbooks and pattern books. The artist or builder was, of course, at liberty to select just what he wanted and could use, and thus it was that the many classical details and ornaments were added to altarpieces or buildings essentially Medieval in structure and design. Usually the most superficial elements of the Renaissance form, such as the decorative ornament, subject matter, and some techniques, were adopted first.

Idealism of the Italian High Renaissance, the expression of emotion and meaning by means of concentration on the human figure, the

Neoplatonic philosophy which sought to derive the universal from the particular and found divine beauty in the idealized corporeal mass was largely misunderstood by the rest of Europe. The northern painter or sculptor tended to move from the Late Gothic style of the fifteenth century directly into the Mannerist style of the mid-sixteenth-century, without a period of codification and idealization. The Late Gothic and Mannerist styles have much in common, the abstraction of forms through elegant elongation, the compression or telescoping of space, the interest in unusual colors and color combinations, and an esoteric symbolism. Thus, Mannerism was congenial outside Italy and found its greatest exponents and fullest expression in the work of el Greco, Holbein, Brueghel, and the School of Fontainebleau. In architecture, after a period of decorative use of classical forms, the Tuscan and Roman classicism in its most austere phase became the norm for the rest of Europe.

Vasari, writing in the sixteenth century, defined the historical period and the new artistic concept of the Renaissance in his biographies of Italian artists. He told how the artists of Tuscany and Rome changed art to the *buona manera antica,* how art was reborn in the manner of the ancients. Vasari's view of his period was shared by Burckhardt three hundred years later, who redefined the period as one in which the splendors, joys, and beauties of the physical world were rediscovered, and the individual man became the focal point of the artist's study and imagination. The period's relation to the ancient world was both general and specific, general in its humanism and idealism, specific in its borrowing of classical forms, motifs, iconography, and decorative details.

The Italians were concerned with the formal philosophy of their art, and Vasari's biographies reflect the changing ideas of the Mannerists on the relationship of art and nature. Nature is constantly varied and constantly changing. It is composed of a mass of details, no two of which are alike. To the Mannerist painter, art seemed an improvement on an ugly, confusing world. Art, being free from life, was free from change, and the appearance of a single perfect moment could be caught forever. Thus, the artist was not content to imitate nature. His aim was to first circumscribe it by codified rules and then to excel it. The study of nature was not an end in itself but an aid to drawing from memory at a later time. The final work of art was to be built on the remembered observation of the most perfect parts of many models which were, in turn, remodelled to conform to the painter's idealized concept of nature.

The dominant role played by the intellect in the art of the sixteenth century was quite different from that which it played in the High

Renaissance. Instead of meticulously observing and recording or interpreting facts, the Mannerist painter isolated himself from the natural world and represented in his art his own theories and emotions. In the typically Mannerist painting, every effect was calculated. Nature was represented in accordance with predetermined rules, rules which were formulated by the artist in his study of the work of other painters as well as the study of his environment. This abstraction of nature is apparent in such diverse paintings as the courtly Mannerism of the School of Fontainebleau, the court portraits of Holbein (Fig. 50), and the academic Mannerism of Antwerp. It is less obvious but certainly also present in the expressive, mystical styles of el Greco (Fig. 53) and Grünewald (Fig. 45).

THE MANNERIST STYLE

A work of art is most surely identified as belonging to the Mannerist school by the artist's use of space in an apparently irrational manner. The Mannerist artist did not feel obliged to obey the laws of perspective, and a completely free variation within the picture was possible. In the early phase of Mannerism, figures were limited to the foreground plane, but they did not seem strained in their relationships. Later, the action was often compressed into a stringently limited area immediately behind the picture plane, and figures were forced to rise upward in an unmotivated manner in order to find accommodation within this very narrow space. The Mannerist artist was not necessarily limited to an intense concentration of energy in the foreground plane. This space was often supplemented by a plunge into depth just as irrational as the suppression of depth. Unlike the spatial effects employed by the artists of the High Renaissance with their symmetrical composition and lines converging at a fairly high vanishing point, the Mannerist artists preferred an asymmetrical composition with a distant vista at one side and a vanishing point placed very low. Usually, the main group of figures occupied the immediate foreground at one side and an expanse of landscape receded endlessly on the other. An impression of depth was gained by sharp contrasts in the scale of figures without the use of elements which produce a linear perspective. The effect is often one of a second narrow panel inserted behind the foreground panel. Elements rationally widely distant were thus juxtaposed in an abrupt telescoping of space.

Closely related to the Mannerist use of space was the Mannerist figure style. At first, a rather ambiguous state seems to exist in which the figures were modelled out as three-dimensional volumes while the space was conceived of as a series of essentially two-dimensional planes; however, a closer examination discloses that the concept of the human figure was as "unreal" as the concept of space. The Mannerist artist sought to excel nature not only by combining the most beautiful parts of various models but also by adding a grace which did not exist in reality. Figures were composed according to a canon of beauty arrived at intellectually rather than by direct observation of the human form, and the figures were conceived in terms of rhythmic linear movements. Parts of the body were fused into a single form as dictated by the composition. Since the poses were contrived for formal elegance or expressive intensity, the gestures and, therefore, the limbs were given greater importance than the torso. The elongated figure became the ideal of physical beauty, since elongation and distortion implied the dematerialization of the flesh. The Mannerist use of the human body as a decorative or expressive medium represented a denial of its physical properties, and the figure finally became a series of undulating surfaces rather than a corporeal mass. If the tangible figure was denied, then the space might just as logically be reduced, and the forms might easily rise upward in their narrow foreground plane. At the same time, the space might be expanded or shifted about and figures juxtaposed with no need to explain their relation in physical terms.

Mannerist composition is characterized by the emphasis on the sides rather than on the center of the work of art and by the use of a serpentine form or line running throughout the work. The surface of a painting may be densely packed with long sinuous figures which are related by rhythmic movements rather than by logical relation in depth through use of perspective. The figures seem to be interlaced on the surface of the painting rather than receding into space; they form adjacent patterns rather than overlapping masses. Although each separate form is related to the picture plane by its position parallel to it and near it, the relation of the forms to each other is often ambiguous.

The Mannerist artist's use of light and color was often a highly personal one. Sometimes, the figures were bathed in an even light which modelled the forms in much the same way that light was used in a Renaissance painting. More often, however, the intensity of the light was constantly and arbitrarily varied into a gliding, flickering pattern. Intense highlights and deep shadows were juxtaposed. Exaggerated reflected light, which brought shadows up to the intensity of the highlights, reduced the apparent spatial requirement of forms and added to the two-dimensional effect of the whole. Mannerist light has been called cold, impersonal, irrational, and even "metaphysical." Colors often did not serve to bring out the form but rather to represent the play of light over it. The Mannerists tended to emphasize primary colors and to juxtapose complimentaries.

Among the courtly aristocratic Mannerist artists, exemplified by the School of Fontainebleau, color did not play a dominant role. Clear, cold colors of light tonality were used with equal intensity throughout the painting, tending to minimize the plasticity of the composition. In the work of the religious, expressive Mannerists, such as El Greco and Grünewald, however, color became a very powerful expressive force. These artists used an illusionistic brush work and large color areas with white highlights, essentially a Venetian technique. The color composition of their paintings was based on a sequence of unconnected color fields in which the large color areas were continued but enlivened with small planes of varying and often inharmonious tones.

The Mannerist ideal spread throughout Europe in the sixteenth century. It did not, however, produce a style as uniform as the International Style of the fourteenth century. Instead, it is a style with wide regional variations based on the artistic traditions developed during the fifteenth century. The period is one of great individual masters rather than uniformly competent schools.

7

Sixteenth-Century Painting
in Germany

ALBRECHT DÜRER AND NORTHERN HUMANISM

The concept of individualism is the key to an understanding of the Northern Renaissance of the sixteenth century. As scholars became increasingly convinced of man's unique status and believed that his position was of primary importance in the Universe, the artist, too, became concerned with individual freedom of expression. The painters looked at the world with fresh eyes and interpreted it in their own way. The scientific attitude toward the study of man and nature which characterized the Renaissance in Italy was less evident in the north. A deep appreciation of nature, resulting in the study and representation of its forms, though rooted in strongly held religious values, was already an important part of northern art in the fifteenth century. The reevaluation of concepts and the manner of representation was characteristic of the sixteenth century.

The Northern Renaissance appeared in each country and region in a somewhat different style. In Germany, the development of art was influenced by the religious and political struggles of the Protestant Reformation. The artist who epitomizes this turbulent period with its profound changes was Albrecht Dürer (1471–1528). Dürer was a Medieval artist in his desire for technical perfection, his unrivalled technique, and his social status as a craftsman, a status against which he protested. He was a Renaissance man in the humanistic breadth of his learning, in his scholarly approach to his subjects, in his independence and defiance of established authority, and in his conception of the artist as a subjective, egocentric genius. He was deeply Christian in spite of the originality of many of his interpretations. Unlike many Italian artists who mixed Christian and pagan concepts, Dürer invested even pagan subjects with a moralistic Christian interpretation. He departed from the artistic traditions of Germany and created new forms based on his studies of the visible world.

In his art, Dürer achieved a classical harmony and clarity, yet never lost interest in detail. His work was always forceful and expressive. Never a very fine colorist, he achieved his fullest personal expression in line, and for the wide dissemination of his ideas, he turned to the graphic arts.

Dürer was born in 1471 in Nuremburg, an important center of art and learning. He was apprenticed to his father, a goldsmith, and later (1486–1489) to Michael Wolgemut, a printmaker whose shop supplied woodcuts for the flourishing printing presses of Nuremburg. At the completion of his apprenticeship, Dürer set off for Colmar to study with Schongauer who died before he arrived in 1487. He moved on to work in Basel, another great printing center, where such humanist works as Brandt's *Ship of Fools* were being published. Back in Nuremburg in 1494, he married Alice Frey and in the same year went to Venice where he studied the work of Mantegna and others. The ten-year period (1495–1505) between his two Italian trips was one of intense productivity for Dürer.

Figure 41. Albrecht Dürer, *The Four Horsemen of the Apocalypse* (published 1498), courtesy of Museum of Fine Arts, Boston, Bequest of Francis Bullard.

Naturally, Dürer's early woodcuts reflected the influence of Wolgemut and the Late Gothic style; however, he went far beyond his master in such works as the *Apocalypse* (1498, Fig. 41) which he published himself. Dürer was concerned with the careful placement of the figures and the definition of solid, individual forms. While he simplified his forms in order to achieve greater clarity of composition, his training as a goldsmith is apparent in the wealth of fine detail. The influence of engraving is also apparent in his greater control, variety of shapes, and skillful use of short, fine lines to give a wider value scale than had hitherto been used in woodcuts. Dürer was familiar with traditional Christian iconography, but he interpreted traditional themes in his own way in keeping with the spirit of the Reformation. He heightened the visionary quality of the *Apocalypse* by contrasting the factual rendering of figures and settings with the unreality of the total image. Thus, in the *Four Horsemen*, the details of bones and flesh, clothing and harness, scales and swords, are all rendered with meticulous care, yet the frightful riders are only in, not of, this world.

At this time, Dürer was painting and engraving. He characterized himself as an artist in his magnificent *Self Portrait* (Munich, 1500). The painting is a true Renaissance portrait—monumental and dignified yet searching and intense, idealized and realistic at the same time. His engravings seem more intimate and refined than either his woodcuts or his paintings. They are personal creations; he executed them himself and prized them above his woodcuts. Dürer studied and admired the engravings of Schongauer but went beyond him in developing a softer, more flowing, richer style.

By the turn of the century, Dürer began to invent new humanistic themes. He was profoundly influenced by Italian Renaissance art with its scientific and classical emphasis. Dürer was constantly studying and borrowing motifs, and almost every figure can be traced to an Italian or classical source during this period. He began to study the nude but still needed a moralistic excuse for its representation. *Adam and Eve* (1504, Fig. 42) is Dürer's first successful synthesis of realism and classical idealism. Adam and Eve face each other symmetrically on each side of the tree and serpent. The idealized figures with their classical profile features and *contrapposto* stance are represented in a naturalistic setting rendered in microscopic detail and filled with symbolic images. Adam almost listlessly touches the Tree of Life in which is perched a parrot, symbolic of true wisdom, while Eve is associated with the Tree of Knowledge and the wily serpent. The cat and mouse at their feet refer to the Fall of Man. The four humors of the body, a late antique theme, are also included—the melancholic elk, the choleric cat for cruelty, the phlegmatic ox for sluggishness, and the sanguine

Figure 42. Albrecht Dürer, *Adam and Eve* (1504),
collection of the Phila-
delphia Museum of Art,
Philadelphia, Pennsylva-
nia.

rabbit for sensual cheerfulness—all in perfect equilibrium in the Garden
of Eden. Dürer's growing self-consciousness as an artist is evident in
the plaque that hangs on the tree with his signature and the date
1504. The intricate and delicate details are made possible by Dürer's
perfection of the engraving technique. When, in 1505, Dürer made a
second trip to Venice, he moved in the highest social circles, a significant
change in public attitude toward the artist. Back in Germany again,
he did a greater number of paintings than before; however, printmaking
remained his most successful mode of expression, and he did his most
significant work in this medium.

The period 1513–1515 is now considered to be the high point of
Dürer's career. In these years, he created his three "master prints,"
Knight, Death, and the Devil, *St. Jerome*, and *Melancholia* (Fig. 43).
In *Knight, Death, and the Devil*, the perfect, stern, self-assured German
knight, whose faith is so strong that temptations are not very real, rides
an equally ideal horse through an eerie landscape where Death appears
on his nag followed by a fantastic demon. The Knight does not struggle
with these phantoms; he simply ignores them. *St. Jerome* shows the
perfect Christian saint in a secluded, tidy cell. In these two master

Figure 43. Albrecht Dürer, *Melancholia* (1515), collection of the Philadelphia Museum of Art, Philadelphia, Pennsylvania.

prints, the Christian struggle for Salvation is represented in two ways: the active life of the knight and the contemplative life of the scholar. The third print in the series, *Melancholia*, symbolizes the limitations of earthly knowledge. A noble figure, surrounded by emblems of learning, is paralyzed by human limitations. The winged, laurel-wreathed figure sits hunched beside a cold, moonlit seaside. *Melancholia*, given its name by the word on the bat-like creature, is filled with intricate ancient, Medieval, and Humanist iconography, dealing with the four humors and with knowledge. The melancholic person was associated with the bat, the dog, and the planet Saturn. The geometric instruments symbolize the artist's interest in scientific knowledge, art theory, perspective, and proportions. Yet, the figure is overcome by lassitude or sheer weariness from fighting insurmountable barriers. The number "1" may refer to the limitation of the artist to the first plane of knowledge, while he wants to advance to the higher level of intuitive thought represented by *St. Jerome*.

During this period, Dürer experimented with a new medium, etching. His first known etching, dated 1513, was inspired by armorers who engraved designs by use of acids. As he drew on the soft wax rather than directly on a metal plate, Dürer achieved a decorative style for creating prints in which the theme, in contrast, is somber if not tragic. The *sudarium* is usually represented as a frontal hieratic image of Christ. Dürer interpreted the theme as one of violent activity with the *sudarium* held by an angel fluttering wildly, and smaller angels holding the instruments of the Passion to stress the suffering of Christ.

Dürer received commissions from Maximilian I until the Emperor's death in 1519. In 1520, he travelled to the Netherlands to see the new Emperor, Charles V, for a renewal of his pension, financing the trip with the sale of his prints in Holland. He kept a careful diary, one of the most valuable documents for the study of the art of the sixteenth century.

During the last period of his life, including his trip to the Netherlands, Dürer was caught up in the Protestant Reformation and was profoundly influenced by Luther. *The Last Supper* (1523), a woodcut, is simple, severe, direct. Its austerity comes not only from a lack of detail but from a determination to capture in art the Protestant point of view. Dürer obviously knew the *Last Supper* by Leonardo da Vinci but chose to represent another moment; the announcement of the betrayal has been made and Judas has left. Christ is surrounded by his faithful disciples, whose unity as a congregation is stressed. The chalice on the table may even be a reminder that, in Protestantism, the layman has the right to receive the wine. Dürer's woodcut is one of the few and certainly the greatest of Protestant representations of the Last Supper.

Dürer was one of the finest watercolorists in the history of western art. He recorded everything that struck his fancy, a piece of turf, a bird's wing, a young hare, with a detailed accuracy reminiscent of the great Flemish masters of the fifteenth century; however, he represented individual objects in nature as a part of a universal whole. Thus, he was able to endow such a simple thing as a clump of weeds with timeless dignity.

That Dürer should produce a magnificent body of drawings is not surprising, considering his work as a graphic artist. His portraits and self portraits are alert and searching, and his drawing of his mother (1514), shortly before her death, is one of the most moving records of the sixteenth century. The *Praying Hands* (Vienna, 1508), a study for the Altarpiece of the Assumption (Heller Altar, destroyed), is delicate and nimble, pulsating with life, a very personal study expressing the northern immediacy of religious response.

Dürer's paintings are seldom as impressive as his prints, for Dürer never became a great colorist. *The Four Apostles* (Munich, 1523–1526,

Figure 44. Albrecht Dürer, *The Four Apostles* (1523–1526), each panel 85 × 30", Bavarian State Painting Collection, Munich, Germany.

Fig. 44) was painted for the city of Nuremburg at a time of religious and political crisis, and to the portraits of John, Peter, Mark, and Paul are added passages from their writings providing spiritual guidance. The two large panels are filled by the figures of Sts. John and Paul; little more than the heads of Sts. Peter and Mark appear beside them. The paintings are deliberately Medieval in their composition. The space is reduced to a narrow stage, and the figures are given no room in which to function. Instead, Dürer concentrated on drapery, the intensity of the gaze, and the expressiveness of the gestures. Nevertheless, the psychological study, the knowledge of anatomy, and the mass and solidity of the forms in spite of their spaceless setting show Dürer to be clearly a man of the Renaissance. In his later years, Dürer devoted increasingly more time to writing on art theory. He died in 1528 in Nuremburg.

MANNERISM IN THE GERMANIC COUNTRIES

A second great master of the Northern Renaissance was Mathias Grünewald (1470/75–1528), called Master Mathias and Mathias Gothardt Neithardt. He was born either in Aschaffenburg or Würzburg and moved from place to place, working in Seligenstadt, Mainz, Frankfurt, and Halle doing sculpture and architecture as well as painting. Grünewald and Dürer were contemporaries and acquaintances; yet they represent opposite poles of the Renaissance in Germany. Whereas Dürer was a humanist trying to achieve an intellectual synthesis of contemporary life and thought with the heritage of both Medieval and classical past, Grünewald approached the world intuitively, following in the traditions of the German mystics. He emphasized the emotional over the intellectual, the subjective or intuitive over the rational in his painting. Dürer expressed himself most effectively in line; Grünewald was a great colorist, using colors for their emotional as well as formal values.

The Isenheim Altarpiece (Colmar, *ca.* 1510–1515, Figs. 45, 46, and 47), painted for the Hospital of St. Anthony, is Grünewald's masterpiece. It was originally composed of a sculptured shrine with double painted wings. When the altar was closed, a brutal painting of the Crucifixion (Fig. 45) was displayed. The painting is a terrifying image of physical and emotional pain based on the writings of St. Bridget of Sweden (1303–1373) in which the physical destruction of Christ is described in vivid terms. The mood of horror and tension is enhanced by the low horizon, the dark almost black sky, the gigantic figure of

Figure 45. Mathias Grünewald, *The Crucifixion* from the Isenheim Altarpiece (closed) (finished 1515), 9'10" × 10'1", Musée Unterlinden, Colmar, France.

Figure 46. Mathias Grünewald, *Madonna and Child* from the Isenheim Altarpiece (finished 1515), 8'10" × 11'2½", Musée Unterlinden, Colmar, France.

Christ with its dripping wounds and decaying flesh, the ghastly colors, and the spiney torturous line. The cross is off-axis, giving an asymmetrical tension to the painting; furthermore, three figures stand on one side, opposing one on the other. Grünewald included St. John the Baptist although St. John was beheaded long before the Crucifixion. Behind him is his prophecy, "He shall increase as I shall decrease." The blood of the Lamb flows into a chalice; thus, Christ sheds His blood for the salvation of mankind. Mary, supported by St. John the Evangelist, is pale and wrapped in a white garment, an image of death. The Mary Magdalene, a tiny figure wringing her hands in despair, personifies physical pain and agony.

On Christmas and Sundays, the outer wings were opened and the *Madonna and Child* (Fig. 46) was revealed in rich glowing colors. On the left, a chorus of angels appears in a flowering Gothic chapel. The angels are represented as almost formless colors, in an attempt to indicate by means of light the essence and not the form of their being. The Madonna, on the other hand, is a realistic German mother seated among the glories of angels in the golden light. The cloth which wraps the Christ Child is ripped and tattered and is the same cloth that covers Him in the Crucifixion; thus, even this moment of greatest joy forecasts the Pietà. Thus, in the visual arts as in their writings, the mystics knew only the extremes of jubilance or agony; there was no middle-ground. On the left of the Madonna is the *Annunciation* and at the right is the *Resurrection* (Fig. 47), the ultimate triumph of Christ. His true being again is pure spirit; therefore, He is represented by pure color, and His body literally is dissolved into light. The whole body is cleansed; the wounds glow in gold and red and His head becomes pure golden light in which the features can scarcely be traced.

Grünewald, more than Dürer, was an early representative of Mannerist tendencies in German art. He used the formal vocabulary of Mannerism in a highly expressive and personal way. His elongated figures, unexplained spatial relations, juxtapositions of contrasting colors and forms, elegant serpentine linear patterns, and mysterious lights often seem a heritage from the fourteenth century rather than a creation of the sixteenth.

Figure 47. Mathias Grünewald, *The Resurrection* from the Isenheim Altarpiece (finished 1515), 8'10" × 4'8¼", Musée Unterlinden, Colmar, France.

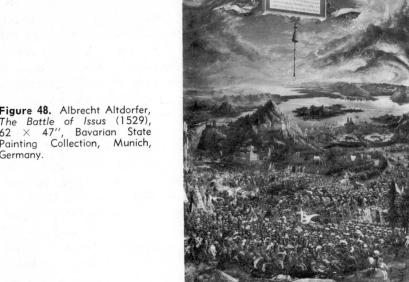

Figure 48. Albrecht Altdorfer, *The Battle of Issus* (1529), 62 × 47″, Bavarian State Painting Collection, Munich, Germany.

The apex of German art was reached in Dürer and Grünewald. Their contemporaries developed one or more aspects of their interests but did not reach their high level of quality and universality. Hans Baldung Grien (1476–1545) was influenced by Dürer and Schongauer. Like most German artists, he was both a painter and a printmaker. He worked in woodcut with the detailed technique developed by Dürer; however, his style is freer, coarser, and less restrained. He liked eerie and fantastic subjects. He preferred slightly elongated figures which he compressed into the foreground; the elegance of his drawing and especially his emphasis on the contours of the forms tended to conflict with the mood of the painting. His colors often have a greenish cast. His paintings, such as *Death and the Maiden* (Basel, *ca.* 1517), are often grotesque or morbid.

Albrecht Altdorfer (1480–1538) lived in Regensburg on the Danube. He was influenced by Grünewald to paint lush panoramas of the Danube Valley. The subject is often incidental, serving as an excuse for painting an untamed forest, a limitless tangle of rough nature. Altdorfer did not paint nature as a series of carefully selected and studied details, but rather he sought to master and reproduce the total impression. The sweep and grandeur of nature has never been portrayed more successfully than in the *Battle of Issus* (Munich, 1529, Fig. 48), which he painted for William IV of Bavaria. The historical episode, the victory of Alexander over Darius, is secondary to the cosmic conflict of the elements themselves; water and fire, sky and earth, the sun and moon, all are included in a sweeping panorama. Color, light, and space are superbly handled.

Lucas Cranach the Elder (1472–1553) became court painter to Frederick the Wise of Wittenberg in 1504–1505, a position which he retained throughout his active, civic life. Cranach was a friend of the leading Humanists and reformers, including both Luther and Dürer. Although he worked with Dürer, Cranach was never as interested in representing accurate perspective or proportions as in achieving a fine decorative effect. He concentrated on perfecting his craftsmanship rather than on new artistic problems. His portraits are simple and direct, although he was more concerned with the type than the individual. Cranach's classical nudes are personal, earthy Venuses, represented without any real concern for ideal proportions. By 1527 he had, in fact, established his own ideal, emphasizing the sinuous contours of enamel-like figures and the contrast of jewels, hats, and transparent draperies with sensuous figures. The *Judgment of Paris* (Karlsruhe, 1530, Fig. 49) is typical of his idealization of the female form and of his delight in still life and landscape painting.

Hans Holbein the Younger (1497–1543) was born in Augsburg, the son of a painter. He moved to Basel by 1515 where he did title pages and illustrations for Moore's *Utopia* and for his friend Erasmus' *In Praise of Folly*. Holbein is best known for his portraits, such as *Erasmus* (Paris, 1523), the most sensitive study of this great Humanist. Holbein's technique was to first make a silver point drawing and then to add light washes and color notes. In the studio, he completed a portrait from memory.

Between 1523 and 1526, Holbein made drawings for the *Dance of Death*, published in 1538 in Lyon. In the finest of the series, *The Farmer*, Holbein visualized Death helping the old man finish plowing the field at the end of the day. These early works show Holbein to be a sensitive, thoughtful Humanist in contrast with the cold aristocratic portraits for which he is best known.

In 1526, Holbein went to England with a letter of introduction from Erasmus to Sir Thomas Moore. In England, he began his great series of court portraits. During his first London visit of two years, he did a series of portraits of Sir Thomas Moore and his family. The portraits of this period are overly elaborate with detailed interior settings. In 1528, Holbein returned to Basel where he found zealous Reformers destroying works of art. The only one of his religious paintings spared

Figure 49. Lucas Cranach the Elder, *The Judgment of Paris* (1530), 13½ × 8¾", Staatliche Kunsthalle, Karlsruhe, Germany.

was the *Basel Altar* because it was too high to reach. Saddened by this turn of affairs, he returned to England where he became court painter to King Henry VIII from 1536 until his death in 1543. Totally objective and noncommital, Holbein painted his subjects against an abstract blue background rather than the natural setting which he had preferred earlier. He filled the space with flat, decorative surface patterns of their costumes from which mask-like faces peer with aloof, aristocratic disdain. Besides portraits of the King, the most famous of which is now in Rome (1540, Fig. 50), he did the triumphal decorations for weddings

Figure 50. Hans Holbein the Younger, *Henry VIII*, (1540), 32½ × 29", Corsini Gallery, National Gallery, Rome, Italy. Photo: Alinari– Art Reference Bureau.

and festivals, painted court portraits, and travelled with King Henry's ambassadors to find another wife for Henry. His paintings of *Christina of Denmark* (London, 1538) and *Ann of Cleves* (Paris, 1539) are the result of these trips. Holbein's style came to dominate northern portrait painting throughout the Renaissance.

8

Sixteenth-Century Painting
Outside Germany

SPANISH PAINTING

In 1519, Charles I of Spain became Holy Roman Emperor as Charles V and under his successors, Philip II and Philip III, Spain became the political center of the Empire. The Spanish sovereigns undertook the defense of the Catholic faith against Protestantism and Spaniards such as Ignatius Loyola, founder of the Jesuit order, were instrumental in the establishment of the Counter Reformation. Artists continued to be employed by the church, not only to enrich its physical structure but also to act as propagandists to stimulate the devotions of the faithful, by emphasizing the miraculous aspects of Christianity in their art. Thus, while Dürer was inspired by the works of the Reformers in Germany and Holland and Holbein was seeing his paintings destroyed in Switzerland, Spanish artists continued to enjoy the patronage of the Catholic church.

Luis de Morales (*ca.* 1500–1586) of Seville is typical. His *Pietà* (Madrid, *ca.* 1570, Fig. 51) is characterized by strong religious feeling, an intimate tender expression, and a lessening of the sculptural quality of modelling and idealized beauty. Morales was influenced by northern Italian painting and the followers of Leonardo da Vinci. Leonardo's influence may be seen in the idealism of the figures and in the accentuated highlights and shadows of the chiaroscuro modelling. Nevertheless, the vertical composition, the compression of space, and the elongated figures are almost Late Gothic in feeling. The emotionalism of the theme is expressed by the Madonna's hands as she clutches Christ, holding the body erect. Morales' very personal style is also a very Spanish style, with its emphasis on the Passion and suffering of Christ. As the Spanish artists lost interest in ideal beauty and turned to religious expressionism with all the emotional intensity of the Counter

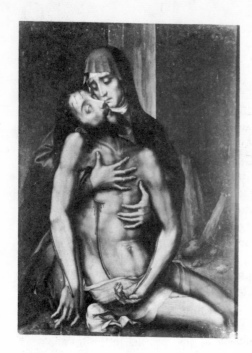

Figure 51. Luis de Morales, *Pietà* (*ca.* 1570), Academy of San Fernando, Madrid, Spain. Photo: Mas.

Figure 52. El Greco, *The Assumption of the Virgin* from Sto. Domingo el Antiguo (1577), 158 × 90", courtesy of the Art Institute of Chicago, Illinois.

Reformation, their paintings became some of the finest examples of religious Mannerism.

One of the greatest of all sixteenth-century artists is Domenikos Theotokopoulos (*ca.* 1541–1614), known as El Greco. He was born in Crete, but about 1560, he went to Venice to study and from there moved to Rome in 1570. By 1577, he had settled in Toledo, Spain. His first important commission was the painting of three altars for the Church of Santo Domingo el Antiguo. The *Assumption of the Virgin* for the high altar (Chicago, 1577, Fig. 52) was influenced in composition and technique by High Renaissance paintings such as Titian's *Assumption* of 1519, but El Greco's personal character emerges in the vigorously contrasting colors, the elongation of proportions, and the emotionalism of the figures. In his early style, El Greco had a strong feeling for the sculpturesque quality of form and extraordinary richness of color. Details of the painting show El Greco's brilliant brush work and skill in the subtle organization of individual parts of the composition.

In *The Burial of Count Orgaz* (Toledo, 1586, Fig. 53) for the Church of Santo Tomé, all aspects of El Greco's mature genius are demonstrated. In the lower half of the painting, the mourners at the funeral, who have become witnesses to the miracle, are contemporary

Figure 53. El Greco, *The Burial of Count Orgaz* (1586), 16′ × 11′10″, Sto. Tomé, Toledo, Spain. Photo: Mas.

Spaniards whose portraits form one of the most remarkably skillful and sensitive depictions of the Spanish physical and psychological type. In the upper half of the canvas is the vision of Christ with St. John and Mary receiving the soul of the Count into glory. When El Greco wished to represent the supernatural, his colors became gray and cold, his drawing nervous and tense, his forms elongated. In Heaven, hard glacial clouds support elongated figures; gray tones are shot with flashes of reds, yellows, and greens; all space is eliminated. Thus he achieved his supernatural effects by denying the normal physical attributes and spatial relationships of objects. A compressed space in the foreground is contrasted with a deep, disconnected space in the Heavens. The composition is unified by the surface patterns created by the flowing arabesque of line leading the eye from stability below to swirling inconsistencies above.

El Greco's late works are typified by the *Laocoön* (Washington, 1610–1614, Fig. 54). The *Laocoön* is a rare example of mythological

Figure 54. El Greco, *Laocoön* (1610–1614), 54⅛ × 67⅞″, National Gallery of Art, Washington, D. C., Samuel H. Kress Collection.

painting by El Greco. Laocoön, the Trojan priest who warned the Trojans against the horse built by the Greeks, is represented with his sons, strangled by serpents. In the distance, the Trojan horse stands in front of the walls of a city which bears a strong resemblance to El Greco's Toledo. The writhing, disembodied figures, almost indistinguishable from the serpents, are "emotional diagrams" rather than living beings. The figures are extremely elongated and are deliberately distorted. In these later paintings, El Greco emphasized the emotional content rather than the objective representation of his subjects. Laocoön is one of the most "expressionistic" of El Greco's works. It shows the extraordinary quality of his imagination, and the originality encouraged by his relatively isolated life in Toledo. The mystical fervor associated with the Spanish temperament and with the Counter Reformation in religion found its finest expression in the painting of this immigrant from Crete who became "more Spanish than the Spaniards."

FRENCH PAINTING

The Renaissance in France was an imported aristocratic style, the result of the individual taste of the monarchs, especially of Francis I. At first, the works of art were sent back by the sovereigns, and then, under Francis I, the artists themselves were brought to France to decorate the royal residences. The most famous visiting artist was Leonardo da Vinci who died in France in 1517. In 1531, Francis began remodelling his palace at Fontainebleau and hired Italians to decorate it in accordance with Renaissance taste. First, Rosso Fiorentino and then Primaticcio (1502–1570) acted as chief architect and decorator for the Chateau at Fontainebleau, completely dominating the royal studios. Even Cellini was in France in the 1530's and 1540's. The Italian masters trained French assistants, and soon a School of Fontainebleau developed. The artists worked as easel painters even on large-scale decorative projects. Paintings on canvas were set into elaborately carved stucco frames on walls and ceilings rather than being executed in fresco. The majority of Fontainebleau artists are now anonymous; they painted mythological and allegorical themes or court portraits.

The French Renaissance is an "anticlassical" style based on Italian Mannerism with convoluted elongations and distortions. Tangible details were used to create an unreal atmosphere, enhancing the French tendency toward over-elegance. The paintings were both decorative and sensuous enough to appeal to an aristocratic taste. The French painters concentrated on surface decoration rather than on mass or form.

Minute realism in details of setting and in portraits was contrasted with an unreal weightless quality in the figure. Compositions and poses were often copied from Italian art.

Portrait painting in France was an aristocratic art, and the portrait of *Francis I* (Paris, 1525–1530, Fig. 55) by Clouet is an excellent example of the style. The royal family required a record of the appearance of its many members and a register of the lineage of the family; thus, albums of drawings and miniatures to be used as jewelry were ordered as well as easel paintings. Francois Clouet's chalk or silver-point portraits of the members of the court are more than mere records of faces and costumes, although they faithfully record surface appearances and are of great documentary value. Clouet used his medium with consummate skill and aristocratic finesse. He is one of the most sensitive draftsmen of any time. The two leading portrait painters in the court of Francis I were Jean (1486–1540) and Francois Clouet (1500–1572). The elegant and aristocratic portraits produced in their shop are not psychological studies but give the substance of the sitter through his wardrobe and surroundings. These paintings are even more decorative than Holbein's court portraits.

Figure 55. Jean Clouet, *Francis I* (ca. 1525–1530), 37¾ × 29″, The Louvre, Paris, France. Photo: Giraudon.

ENGLISH PAINTING

History of painting in England is principally the story of foreign artists—Hans Holbein, Antoninus Mor, Frederico Zucaro, and Peter Paul Rubens. These artists founded no schools and produced only a handful of imitators. On the other hand, the English nobles were patrons of the arts in a different sense. They assembled great art collections which, however, fostered connoisseurship rather than creative activity. The only regular commissions in the sixteenth century were portraits. In the first quarter of the century, the field was dominated by Hans Holbein. Toward the end of the reign of Henry VIII, Holbein's influence was superseded by a group of inferior Flemish painters; by the end of Edward VI's reign, the Flemish influence was dominant. Only one Flemish painter of distinction visited England in the Tudor period— Antoninus Mor. Mor probably accompanied Philip II of Spain on his trip to England for his wedding with Mary I in 1554.

Typical paintings of the Elizabethan period were essentially decorative. Court painters were fashion illustrators rather than portrait painters. Portraits of Queen Elizabeth fail to capture her remarkable personality and, instead, concentrate on the decorative details of her costume.

The finest English painting of the age was the work of miniaturists such as Nicholas Hilliard (1537-1619). Hilliard's style combines Medieval miniature painting with the portrait style of Holbein. The *Youth Leaning Against a Tree* (London, 1588) or *George Clifford, Earl of Cumberland* (Kansas City, 1590-1592, Fig. 56), though small in scale, show all the skill and sensitivity of a Holbein. Hilliard had a masterful technique, a penetrating insight into character, and a taste for cool, gracious representations.

Figure 56. Nicholas Hilliard, *George Clifford, Earl of Cumberland* (1590–1592), oval 2 3/4 × 2 3/16″, Nelson Gallery-Atkins Museum (Gift of the Starr Foundation), Kansas City, Missouri.

NETHERLANDISH PAINTING

During the sixteenth century, Antwerp developed into the economic center of the Netherlands; thus, it, rather than Bruges or Brussels, became the Renaissance city of Flanders. To satisfy the demand for art from the newly rich burghers, paintings were produced rapidly. The style is now commonly called "Antwerp Mannerism" because of its blending of Flemish and Italian Mannerist characteristics.

Quentin Massys (*ca.* 1465–1530), or Matsus or Metsys, typifies the best of the Antwerp School. He was born in Louvain and as a student was influenced by the paintings of Dirk Bouts and Roger van der Weyden. He lived and worked in Antwerp from 1491 until his death in 1530. He was a friend of the Humanists, Sir Thomas Moore, Erasmus, and Holbein. In the Altarpiece of St. John (Brussels, 1508–1511), the Lamentation was inspired by Van der Weyden's *Deposition*. It is flanked by Salome holding the head of John the Baptist and John the Evangelist being boiled in oil. Massys was fascinated by semi-Oriental costumes and grotesque facial types which he represented with detailed realism. He had a fine feeling for delicate colors and surface patterns rather than interrelationships in space. His paintings have a crowded composition and rapid linear rhythms often inappropriate to somber themes. Massys' strength lay in his sensitivity in the representation of subdued grief and controlled stillness. His weakness was in his self-conscious striving for refinement.

Acknowledged leader of the Antwerp Mannerists was Jan Gossart, called Mabuse (1470/80–*ca.* 1536), the court artist of Philip of Burgundy. His *Neptune and Amphitrite* (Berlin, 1516) is the earliest documented painting of life-sized nudes in the north. Mabuse was very proud of his "enlightenment" and his classical knowledge; however, his paintings tend to be cold and sculptural studies. Mabuse was a great innovator and typical Mannerist in his attempt to surpass his models in both realism and decorative quality. The *Madonna with Saints* (Palermo, after 1511) was one of his greatest projects, superbly executed in a brilliant, ornamental style. The spiritual conception of the theme is of secondary interest to the artist, whose chief concern was with the representation of cubic volumes in space and the creation of luxurious, decorative effects.

Joachim Patenier (*ca.* 1475–1524), a member of the Antwerp painters' guild after 1515, was the first Fleming to devote himself to landscape painting. Figures, often painted by other artists such as Massys, were simply an excuse to paint landscape and supplied the title, the *Tempta-*

tion of St. Anthony (Madrid), for example. Patenier was interested in geography; he surveyed the landscape from above and painted great topographical vistas in accurate aerial perspective.

Fashionable painting in the second half of the sixteenth century was dominated by Bernard van Orly (*ca.* 1488–1541), the court painter for both Margaret of Austria and Mary of Hungary. It is his name that is most closely associated with the whole development of Antwerp Mannerism and the Renaissance style in Belgium. He painted portraits and altarpieces and made designs for tapestries and stained glass. Van Orly was one of the leading "Romanists" in the Netherlands. An admirer of Raphael, he may have visited Italy and certainly could have studied the great Raphael tapestry cartoons when they were in Brussels (1515–1519). He also met Dürer when he visited the Netherlands in 1520.

An Antwerp painter who rose above the local school and stands alone as one of the unique figures in the history of art is Peter Brueghel the Elder (1522/30–1569). Brueghel is first mentioned in the Antwerp list of painters in 1551. He worked for a publisher, Jerome Cock, in Antwerp, reproducing Bosch paintings as prints, and it is there that he learned the style and iconography of Bosch. He visited Italy and France about 1553, but he was more impressed by the landscape than by the art. Brueghel's first independent works were skillfully executed didactic prints of virtues, vices, and proverbs, influenced by Erasmus' concept of the folly and knavery of man. The virtues and vices are represented in everyday terms as morals and customs, the hypocrisy practiced by Everyman. In his drawing, *The Large Fishes Eat the Little Ones* (Vienna), Brueghel illustrated a proverb and also showed the natural condition of man.

In Brueghel's paintings of peasants and landscapes, the peasant represented Everyman. Brueghel was not interested in the individual, and he never painted portraits. His figures are rather squat, usually seen from above; they are clumsy yet agile. The solid drawings are filled with brilliant local color which intensifies their silhouettes. Brueghel's compositions are organized around a central focal point which is often not immediately apparent because of his rather tapestry-like effects. Thus, in the *Wedding Dance* (Detroit, *ca.* 1565, Fig. 57), the white aprons and kerchiefs of the women and the dashes of red-orange in the costumes of both men and women lead the eye in a serpentine fashion back through the landscape and up over the surface of the painting. The banquet table, with its drape of honor and crown, are lost at the upper edge of the painting, while the woman jigging in the center of the crowd, by virtue of the intensity of the color and decorative outlines of her draperies, forms the focal point of the composition.

Brueghel's landscapes, in the tradition of Patenier and Altdorfer, are among his finest work. The landscapes typify a new type of Christian pantheism in which the earth became the basic element, and nature was an animate, living soul. The earth had moods and feelings as well as life, and the weather expressed these moods of nature. Nature was never seen by Brueghel as the destroyer, but as the life-giving force,

Figure 57. Peter Brueghel the Elder, *The Wedding Dance* (1568), 47 × 62″, courtesy of the Detroit Institute of Arts, Michigan.

and as such, he represented it in a great series of the months, only five of which survive. December with *Hunters in the Snow* (Vienna, *ca.* 1568, Fig. 58) shows one of nature's moods, cold and icy with an overcast sky, still, crisp air, black trees, and huts and houses blanketed

under snow. Brueghel paints with his own individual interpretation of
the Mannerist style. The curvilinear distortion of dogs and men, the
verticality and elongation of trees and roofs, the sharp contrast of foreground and far distance, the asymmetrical balance of the composition,
the elegance of the drawing, and the reduction of color are all part of
the Mannerist aesthetic.

A similar composition is used in *The Fall of Icarus* (Brussels,
Fig. 59), Brueghel's only surviving mythological painting. Even here,

Figure 58. Peter Brueghel the Elder, *Hunters in the Snow* (1565),
46 × 63¾", Kunsthistorisches Museum, Vienna, Austria.

the activities of men are subordinate to nature, and a classical subject
is made to serve a broader purpose. The painting appears to be concerned with a plowman, a shepherd, and a fisherman. The classical
story of Icarus is combined with a Dutch proverb which says "No plow
stops at a death"; the head and corpse of a dead man in the bushes
can be seen at the left. Unobserved in the distance, Icarus plunges into
the sea. The theme of the painting is not only the fall of pride, but it

Figure 59. Peter Brueghel the Elder, *The Fall of Icarus*, (1568), 24½ × 44″, Royal Museum, Brussels, Belgium. Photo: Copyright A.C.L., Brussels.

is a warning that even the death of the great or daring man is unobserved. The fate of one man does not alter a nature in which the individual part is insignificant. It has been suggested that the ship leading to the sun may be a symbol for the Church, and the people performing their daily tasks, a symbol of the Christian's hope for salvation through faithful performance of duty.

9

Sixteenth-Century
Sculpture and Architecture

A study of sixteenth-century art outside Italy would not be complete without some discussion of sculpture and architecture. The architects and sculptors are not as well known as the painters; nevertheless, their contribution to the history of art is just as significant. Too often, they are bypassed as the student turns from the great cathedrals of the Gothic period to the palaces and churches of Italy in the Renaissance and Baroque periods. This brief chapter can only serve to indicate the general tendencies and a few high points of the sixteenth century, mainly in France, Spain, and England.

FRENCH SCULPTURE

French sculpture was profoundly influenced by the bronze replicas of famous ancient sculptures made by Primaticcio for the French court about 1542. These "antiques" together with the Italianate sculpture that was being produced at Fontainebleau were the source of style and iconography for the French sculptors of the sixteenth century. The finest sixteenth-century sculptor was Jean Goujon (died *ca.* 1568) whose most important work was produced as architectural decoration. The nymphs on the *Fountain of the Innocents* (Paris, 1548–1549) are graceful feminine forms whose clinging drapery and fine fluttering folds are reminiscent of Neo-Attic work of the Hellenistic period in Greece. At the same time, the Mannerist compression of space and elongation of figures is seen throughout his work. About 1550, he was employed on the Louvre, where he executed the pairs of allegorical figures framing the windows in the third story of Pierre Lescot's façade (Fig. 63). The wall surface is covered with elegant idealized figures, elongated and twisted into serpentine poses according to the Mannerist ideal. The source of indi-

95

vidual details is unquestionably Italian, but the cold, crisp, linear quality of the sculpture is clearly French.

A second court sculptor of the French Renaissance was the Parisian, Germain Pilon (1535–1590). Although influenced by Goujon, his style reflects the *détente* of the fifteenth century. The Virtues on the *Monument for the Heart of Henry II* are close to the Goujon feminine ideal. Pilon executed the sculpture of the *Mausoleum of Henry II* (St. Denis, 1563–1570) designed by Primaticcio. The kneeling bronze portraits and the marble cadavers of the King and Queen are in his naturalistic vein. Later, he even returned to Medieval polychroming; sometimes, his work seems almost Spanish in its realism and expressionism.

SPANISH SCULPTURE

Spanish Renaissance sculpture was first dominated by Italian artists. Domenico Fancelli (1469–1519), a Florentine, came to Spain in 1510 and designed the double Tomb of Ferdinand and Isabel in the Royal Chapel at Granada (1514–1517). This introduction of Italian forms and details was influential in the development of native sculptors such as Diego de Siloe (1490/95–1563). Siloe studied in Italy and, on his return to Spain, built the *Golden Stair* for the Cathedral of Burgos (1519–1523), based on Bramante's design for the Belvedere court of the Vatican Palace. The remarkable sense of calligraphic movement and surface ornament seen in the stone reliefs and metal work of the stair are characteristic of the style known as a Renaissance Plateresque. In 1528, Diego de Siloe went to Granada where he was in charge of the building of the Cathedral.

Alonso Berruguete (*ca.* 1489–1561), son of Pedro Berruguete, was the leading Spanish master of the Renaissance. Alonso was a highly individual and very Spanish artist. Trained in Italy, he returned to Spain in 1518 and settled in Valladolid as court artist for Charles V. His altarpiece of San Benito (Valladolid, 1526–1532), of polychromed and gilded wood, was composed of figures set into niches forming a huge triumphal arch. The individual figures are characteristically Spanish in their extreme emotionalism and intentional distortions into angular, tortured forms. The realism of the modelling contrasts with the gilding of the drapery, the hair, and the landscape which deny this very realism and turn the figure into something inhuman and decorative. Berruguete's masterpieces are the low relief carvings in the backs for the choir stalls in the Toledo Cathedral (1539–1548, Fig. 60). These figures come close to a classical expression of ideal physical beauty and harmonious proportions. Both *Adam* and *Eve* illustrate the heroic,

Figure 60. Alonso Berruguete, *Eve*, Choir Stalls (1539–1548), 31½ × 19¼″, Cathedral, Toledo, Spain. Photo: Mas.

muscular canon of beauty preferred by Berruguete. The nude female figure is rarely represented in Spanish art. Even more unusual is the idealized beauty of the figure of Eve. The monumental conception of the figure is based on Michelangelo's art, but the elegant stance and sinuous contours are characteristically Mannerist. The emphasis on grace is more apparent here than in most of Berruguete's work. The inter-twining of woman, tree, and serpent, the compression of the forms into a narrow foreground plane, and the establishment of a rectangular frame for the composition only to break it with the head, hand, and thigh of Eve are all typical Mannerist conceits. A similar composition was used in other figures, such as *St. John the Baptist*, to achieve an emotional impact. Superhuman but emaciated figures, neither sitting nor standing, were elegantly imprisoned in a space impossibly small. Berruguete's sculpture is closely related to El Greco's painting. He, too, was an expressionist who often denied physical beauty in the in-terests of expressionism. The Italianate architectural elements surrounding the figures with their low relief carving of candelabra, swags, trophies, and grotesques add to the sense of over-elegant refinement and instability.

Juan de Juni (1507–1577) was French by birth but settled in Val-ladolid and, like El Greco, became more Spanish than the Spaniards. His *Entombment* (Valladolid, 1541–1544) in polychromed wood emphasizes the suffering of Christ and His followers. The composition is a symmetrical group with evenly spaced figures. The heads are based on the classical canon of beauty. The total effect, however, is one of unrestrained emotion. Even the drapery expresses the violence in its mass of angular folds. This emotionalism is characteristic of Spanish sculpture during the sixteenth century.

In the second half of the sixteenth century, a new influx of Italian artists occurred during the work on Philip II's Escorial. The group was led by the Milanese, Pompeo Leone (1533–1608), who executed the High Altar and Tombs of Charles V and Philip II (1571–1591) in the Escorial in a very strict Late Renaissance form.

GERMAN AND NETHERLANDISH SCULPTURE

The finest German Renaissance sculpture was executed in bronze, and the name most often associated with sixteenth-century bronzes is that of the Vischer family of Nuremburg. Herman the Elder (died 1488) established a bronze foundry in Nuremburg in 1453. His son, Peter (ca. 1450–1529), took over the shop at his father's death, and

Figure 61. Vischer Family, *Shrine for the Reliquary of St. Sebald* (1507–1519), Church of St. Sebald, Nuremburg, Germany. Photo: Mader.

his five sons in turn continued the family tradition through the sixteenth century. The *Shrine for the Reliquary of St. Sebald* in Nuremburg (1507–1519, Fig. 61) is the Vischers' most important work. The tomb-like reliquary, with its elaborate Late Gothic building, is Medieval in conception; however, an attempt was made to give individual figures, such as the Apostles, some of the idealized grace and elegance of Italian art. The best characteristics of the Vischers and the German Renaissance are found in their forceful realism, vigorous modelling, and restrained taste.

In the second half of the sixteenth century, northern European sculpture was dominated by Flemish and Dutch artists working under the influence of Giovanni da Bologna. Hubert Gehrhardt (1545–1620) combined the Italian manner with Dutch love of massiveness in fountains in Augsburg and Munich. Adrian de Vries of the Hague (1560–1627) produced a fine series of small bronzes whose muscular, elaborate poses show him to be a faithful follower of Giovanni da Bologna. His best works are the *Fountain of the Flying Mercury* and the *Hercules and Hydra Fountain* at Augsburg.

ENGLISH SCULPTURE

The figurative arts in England during the Renaissance suffered from the Puritanical influence of the Reformation and from the domination of patronage by foreigners. A debased Gothic style was in general use throughout the sixteenth century. The tombs of Henry VII and his mother, Margaret, Countess of Richmond, both in the Henry VII Chapel in Westminster Abbey, are among the handsomest surviving works; however, they are by Pietro Torregiano of Florence (1472–1528) who worked in England between 1512 and 1526.

FRENCH ARCHITECTURE

Renaissance architecture in France falls into two periods, an early composite style found principally in the Loire Valley and, later, a full Italianate style. The Loire Valley style is based on a combination of Medieval structural principles and Renaissance decoration. In the Francis I wing at the Chateau at Blois (1515–1519), classical details are used throughout, but the design is governed by function rather than by the ideal of symmetry of the Italian Renaissance. The famous open spiral staircase is actually a Gothic newel staircase whose asymmetrical placement enhances the irregularity of the plan. The rich applied decoration is composed of classical foliage and mouldings.

The Chateau at Chambord (1526–1544, Fig. 62), a hunting lodge ordered by Francis I, was built on a symmetrical Renaissance plan. The central building is set in a great court with four corner turrets on both outer and inner walls, and the lodge is a Greek cross with a staircase in the center. At a distance, the building with its chimneys, steep roofs, and turrets has an irregular, picturesque quality that is quite Medieval. On closer inspection, it becomes apparent that classical ornament has been substituted for Gothic in decorative sculpture and mouldings. The two styles remain in conflict, a confusion of individually handsome details.

After about 1540, more Italian artists came to France, and French artists used Italian forms with greater understanding. Serlio and Vignola both worked for the court, and their books on architecture were published in Lyon. Thus, the mature French Renaissance style is derived from the restrained academic phase of Italian Renaissance architecture. Philibert L'Orme (ca. 1510–1570), the son of a master mason of Lyon, studied in Italy and, in 1567, published a book on architecture himself. He did not advocate the unimaginative copying of ancient and Italian Renaissance buildings but intended to adapt the Renaissance style to the climate, traditions, and materials of France. His concern was with practical matters, the orientation of the building, the function of the

Figure 62. Chateau at Chambord (begun 1519, 1526–1544), France, Photo: Archives Photographiques.

rooms, and methods of construction. The Chateau at Anet (1548–1554), which he designed for Diane de Poitiers, was demolished, but one wing, a gate, and a chapel survive. Its typically French plan included a living area set back behind a court of honor, and side wings extended from the main building. A screen wall with a central pavilion shielded the complex from the road. Formal gardens extended behind the living area. The main gate at Anet is an adaptation of a triumphal arch elaborated with balconies, interlacing balustrades, a deer on the top of the pediment in reference to Diana the Huntress, and a relief of the reclining Diana in the tympanum. The sculpture, by Cellini, is now in the Louvre.

Rebuilding of the palace of the Louvre was the greatest building project of the period. Pierre Lescot (1510–1578) was given full charge of the Louvre in 1546 (Fig. 63). He planned a building with side wings, a court of honor, and a monumental gateway with screen walls, of which the west side of the main block in the south wing was built. The three pavilions with engaged pilasters of columns are typically French in their vertical emphasis; however, the building is essentially horizontal, and the roof, though visible, has been lowered. A triumphal arch motif and pedimented windows are used throughout with thorough knowledge of Renaissance detail. First floor windows are recessed, creating an arcade motif. The sculptural decoration by Goujon unites the architectural elements, producing a graceful surface over the building. The Louvre, as planned, had very handsome proportions, large but not

Figure 63. Pierre Lescot, Louvre (Lescot's work begun 1546), Paris, France. Photo: Archives Photographiques.

overwhelming. Typically Renaissance was the balance, humanistic scale, and formal rhythmic variations. The upper story of the south wing was added in the seventeenth century, providing an instructive contrast with its ungainly, though more accurately classical, details.

SPANISH ARCHITECTURE

Spanish architecture, too, can be divided into two phases: the Early Renaissance (1500–1560) is also often referred to as Renaissance Plateresque because of the architectural use of rich low relief ornament; and the Late Renaissance or Herreran style (1560–1600/10), which was created by Juan de Herrera for the Escorial.

The Cathedral of Granada (begun in 1523, Fig. 64) was the major building project of the early Spanish Renaissance. The sanctuary is a Renaissance adaptation of the plan of the Church of the Holy Sepulchre by Diego de Siloe who took over the project in 1528. The design of the interior elevation and the north transept façade is a classical one, based on the triumphal arch motif. Classical orders are used throughout. On the interior, compound piers have high bases and a full entablature which is used like a stilt block. The vault of the nave is of Late Gothic form with decorative ribs. Coffered barrel vaults surround the rotunda

Figure 64. Diego de Siloe, Cathedral of Granada (1523, 1528 and later), Spain. Photo: Mas.

Figure 65. Juan de Herrera, The Escorial (after 1559), Spain. Photo: Mas, by permission of the Patrimonio Nacional.

sanctuary. The Cathedral of Granada is a handsome, elegant building. The sobriety of ornament is probably due to Diego's Italian training.

The Palace of Charles V, placed directly on the grounds of the Moorish palace, the Alhambra, in Granada, was begun by Pedro Machuco in 1527. The Palace is a severe classical building. All sides of the building are exactly alike, heavily rusticated walls with the Doric order below and the Ionic above, relieved by sculptured medallions and circular windows flanking central portals. The exterior surface composition is related neither to the function nor to the interior disposition of the rooms of the building. A circular courtyard is placed in the center of this square building, another indication of the architect's concern with form rather than the function of the building.

The Late Renaissance, or Herreran style, appeared during the last forty years of the century and was derived from Juan de Herrera's masterpiece, the Escorial (1559, Fig. 65), built for Philip II. Philip was fanatically devout and ordered a monastery, church, palace, and tomb combined in one building. The complex was laid out as a symmetrical gridiron plan, perhaps in reference to the martyrdom of its patron St. Lawrence, with the church on the central axis. The Greek cross plan of the church itself was derived from St. Peter's in Rome as was the use of the triumphal arch motif in the nave arcade. The

Doric order was used in the church interior. On the façade, the Ionic order in the second story contrasts with the extremely severe Doric below. The Mannerist tendencies of the second half of the sixteenth century are apparent in the overwhelming scale of the complex and in the top-heavy appearance of the church. More classical in feeling are the cloisters with their central tempietto. Herrera and the Escorial dominated Spanish architectural thinking well into the Baroque period.

ENGLISH ARCHITECTURE

The Tudor Period (1471–1547) began as an extension of the Perpendicular Style into the sixteenth century. Tudor religious architecture culminated in the Henry VII Chapel at Westminster Abbey (Fig. 66), built between 1503 and 1519 by the architects Robert (died 1506) and William Vertue (flourished 1500–1527). The architects conceived of the building in terms of mass, not space; its effect of richness is derived from the repetition of similar forms, not by inventiveness in

Figure 66. Robert and William Vertue, Chapel of Henry VII (1503–1519), Westminster Abbey, London, Photograph supplied by the Church Information Board and reproduced by the courtesy of the Dean and Chapter of Westminster.

decorative detail. Inside and out, a single unified effect resembling wood paneling is achieved through the use of stone tracery over walls, buttresses, and windows. The windows are set on angles, as are the buttresses, to break up the surfaces. The Chapel is covered by pendant fan vaults in which the vault is held in place by the weight of interior pendants at the haunches and key stones, although the usual technique of buttressing on the exterior is also used. The force of gravity is used against itself, and the traditional principles of Medieval building are reversed in a spectacular display of craftsmanship. By the end of the Tudor Period, Italian Renaissance motifs began to be used; however, the structural forms were still those of the Perpendicular Style.

In secular architecture, too, the late Medieval style survived long after Italian forms dominated architecture on the continent. In the sixteenth century, some of the finest Medieval homes were erected; for example, Compton Wynyates, built about 1520, is a typical English manor house which owes nothing to the Renaissance. It has an irregular picturesque quality with steep roofs and battlemented towers grouped around the great hall and central courtyard. The use of contrasting materials, bricks, stone, timber, and plaster is characteristically English. The large windows are derived from the Perpendicular phase of the Late Gothic, and the bay windows are an especially English feature. Compton Wynyates is a comfortable house whose style is based on the requirements of climate and English country life as well as on artistic tradition.

Hampton Court Palace (1515–1540) was built for Cardinal Woolsey who later gave it to Henry VIII as a royal palace. The entrance has battlemented towers and pointed arches, ornamental patterns in the brick wall, a conglomeration of chimneys, and an oriel window over the front door. The first hint of the Renaissance is found in the entrance towers where medallions with classical busts of Roman emperors done by Italian craftsmen in England were placed. The plan is purely Medieval with courtyard and a great hall. Huge Late Gothic windows contrast with the decoration of the wall with the busts of Roman emperors.

In the second half of the sixteenth century, the Elizabethan period, the architects became increasingly aware of their European neighbors and produced an exuberant architecture showing much more Renaissance influence. The country house was the most important architectural form. Longleat (1567–1580) may have been designed by an Italian architect, John of Padua. Its Renaissance character is seen in its horizontal composition and use of superimposed classical orders, balustrades, and an entrance portico. Although the design is correct and symmetrical, the large mullioned windows, projecting bays, and clustered chimneys are reminiscent of earlier English buildings.

Wollaton Hall (1580–1588, Fig. 67) resembles Longleat only in its sturdy square shape, clear division of the stories, and large windows. Italian Renaissance regularity has disappeared in the exuberant conglomeration of architectural details from a variety of continental sources. The great hall is placed in the center of the complex and is emphasized with a tower instead of the usual courtyard. Angle towers are almost

Figure 67. Wollaton Hall (1580–1588), Nottingham, England. Photo: By courtesy of the Nottingham Corporation.

detached in the French manner. Decorative coupled columns with a niche between them reflect the influence of Lescot's Louvre, and pepperpot turrets resemble designs by Philibert L'Orme. The influence of Dutch pattern books can be found in bands which break the middle of the columns and in pilasters and obelisk used as roof decoration. Highly ornate strap work, flat decorative patterns, and ornamental gables are also derived from north European architecture. The building is typically Mannerist in its capriciousness and extravagance; however, most Tudor buildings are less extreme than Wollaton Hall.

Architecture, among the visual arts, best expresses the spirit of the Elizabethan age, and only architecture approaches the brilliance of the Elizabethan literary and political activity. Elizabethan art is eclectic on the one hand but both imaginative and functional on the other. Artists were exploring the world and creating new forms from a mixture of past and distant styles. The new hopes and desires of the age of exploration demanded an architecture that was based on the past yet flexible and adaptable for the future. If at times the style seems chaotic and without direction, at least it is bold and experimental. Thus, with the Elizabethan period, the artists and architects are firmly established in the modern world.

index

Renaissance Art Outside Italy

MARILYN STOKSTAD. Professor Marilyn Stokstad is chairman of the Department of the History of Art at the University of Kansas. She received her B. A. degree from Carleton College, M. A. from Michigan State, and Ph. D. from the University of Michigan. She has held a Fulbright Fellowship to Norway and an A. A. U. W. Fellowship to Spain.

THE art horizons SERIES

- **CLASSICAL ART** R. L. Bohr, Sacramento State
- **THE ART OF THE ITALIAN RENAISSANCE** Edmund Eglinski, University of Kansas
- **MODERN ART: THE NINETEENTH AND TWENTIETH CENTURIES** John C. Galloway, Oakland University, Rochester, Michigan
- **FORMS OF ART** Peter Gilleran, Wayne State University, Detroit
- **AMERICAN ART** David Gebhard, University of California, Santa Barbara
- **VISUAL ART IN GLASS** Dominick Labino
- **POTTERY** Charles Lakofsky, Bowling Green State University
- **ASIAN ART** John D. LaPlante, Stanford University
- **THE ART OF THE PRINT** Earl G. Mueller, Duke University
- **ART IN COMMERCE AND INDUSTRY** Robert C. Niece, Art Center College of Design, Los Angeles, California
- **ANCIENT ART** Robert H. Rough, Michigan State University
- **MEDIEVAL ART** Norris K. Smith, Washington University
- **SEVENTEENTH AND EIGHTEENTH CENTURY ART** Robert Stinson, Bowling Green State University
- **RENAISSANCE ART OUTSIDE ITALY** Marilyn Stokstad, University of Kansas
- **PREHISTORIC ART** Frederick O. Waage, Cornell University
- **CRAFTS AND CRAFTSMEN** Irwin Whitaker, Michigan State University
- **PHOTOGRAPHY**

WM. C. BROWN COMPANY PUBLISHERS

Dubuque, Iow

DATE DUE

NO 26 '68			
FE 9 '69 FE 1 '69			
MY 9 - '69			
MO 12 '69 FE 25 72			
MY 13 '73			
MR 5 74			
JA 6 - '75			
MY 18 '77 MR 2 1981			
APR 15 1982 OCT 26 '90			
NOV 25 '91			
DEC 06 '91			
FEB 9 '94			
			PRINTED IN U.S.A.
89			